From Beardstown to Andersonville

The Civil War Letters of Newton Paschal and Tommy Paschal

A Special Edition in Commemoration of the 150th Anniversary of the Civil War

by
Joseph Edward Fulton

HERITAGE BOOKS
2011

HERITAGE BOOKS

AN IMPRINT OF HERITAGE BOOKS, INC.

Books, CDs, and more—Worldwide

For our listing of thousands of titles see our website
at
www.HeritageBooks.com

Published 2011 by
HERITAGE BOOKS, INC.
Publishing Division
100 Railroad Ave. #104
Westminster, Maryland 21157

International Standard Book Numbers
Paperbound: 978-0-7884-5331-1
Clothbound: 978-0-7884-8789-7

This book is dedicated to my loving wife Debra Lynn Hascall, whose own great-great grandfather, James Hascall, defied the popular sentiment in the border state of Missouri and fought for the Union Army as part of the 39th Missouri Volunteer Infantry. Hascall survived a battle against the notorious Quantrill Raiders and died in 1922 at the age of 81.

Acknowledgements

If she were alive today my first thanks would go to my great-grand-mother, Mary Paschal Hobson, who carefully preserved these letters from her two brothers, a boyfriend and a cousin who served the Union in the Civil War. The letters went virtually unnoticed and forgotten for more than a century as they passed from Mary to my grandmother, Clara Hobson Fulton; my father, Charlton Paschal Fulton and finally my sister, Mary Fulton, who passed the letters on to me as a 40th birthday present in 1994. By having the letters published I can at least assure that they will never again be hidden away and forgotten.

I would like to thank my student assistants, Lorcy Billings and Hannah Archambault; Marvin Pace of the Library of Congress; William Talkemeyer of the Cass County, Illinois Historical Society; Susan Moreland of the Jacksonville, Illinois Municipal Building; Mary Smith of the Chapin, Illinois Historical Society; Bill Fisher of the 114th Illinois Re-Enactment Regiment and Dorothy Allen, a genealogist from Normal, Illinois.

Above all I would like to thank my cousin Donna Hess Cooper, whose shared Paschal lineage and extensive genealogical research proved indispensable to this book.

Table of Contents

Introduction

Two brothers, Asa Newton Paschal and Samuel Thomas Paschal, wrote the letters included in this volume during and shortly following the American Civil War. They offer a rare and honest insight into the realities of two common farm boys who abandoned the safety and simplicity of their home near Beardstown, Illinois to risk and, in Newton's case, sacrifice, their lives for flag and Union. Their sister, Mary Elizabeth Paschal Hobson, lovingly preserved these letters that were passed on to her daughter Clara Hobson Fulton and are now in the protective care of Clara's grandson, the editor of this book.

Asa Newton Paschal of Company A, 114th Regiment, Illinois Volunteer Infantry wrote sixty-three of the letters. Newton fought at Vicksburg and was captured at Brice's Cross Roads. He died at Andersonville. Thirty-three letters were written in the first nine months following the war by Samuel Thomas Paschal, Company F, 47th Regiment, Illinois Volunteer Infantry, while he was stationed in Alabama with other Union troops to protect the tenuous peace. Tommy fought at Spanish Fort and Fort Blakley during the siege of Mobile.

The juxtaposition between the letters of these two brothers is one of the more intriguing aspects of this meticulously preserved collection. Much of the difference lies in their ages. Newton's letters were written when he was between 24 and 26 years of age, having previously traveled to other states and having attained a more formal education than his younger brother Tommy. Newton did not lack confidence in his ability to relate to the fairer sex. He knew he was "pretty good lookin" and remembers to send his regards to the girls in the neighborhood.

Tommy, on the other hand, was only 16 when he enlisted in the 47th Illinois Regiment after Newton's death. He was relatively inexperienced in worldly ways, unschooled, and uncommonly shy. He comments in one letter that "thare is a good meney girls in this city but, as you know, I am afraid of the girls. I havent spoke to one of them yet." However, at other times, one hears the echo of Newton's thoughts, beliefs and actions, and Tommy attempts the braggadocio of Newton. This is most obvious in Newton's attitude toward the negro and those of other nationalities different from him. Newton's words reveal a deep and inherent prejudice, while Tommy's words seem to merely echo those of Newton without containing the sincerity of a firm conviction.

The brothers did, however, share a strong devotion to their family, particularly sister Mary. They were frequently generous, often compassionate, brave and capable of humor in the worst of times. They worried about the crops at home, took a special interest in the flora of the South, and expressed their delight in its beauty and appreciation of its bounty.

Different from many diaries that were often written with the view toward public access, and sometimes edited by the writer before release, the letters of Newton and Tommy were written to family members, with no thought that they would be read by anyone other than the person to whom they were addressed. Consequently they candidly convey the sentiments of the writers, and we have made no effort to alter the language or opinions expressed. Spelling remains as set forth in the letters as much as we could ascertain the spelling. Newton's penmanship was good but haste and writing conditions no doubt contributed to the misspellings and word omissions.

On the contrary, Tommy's penmanship was poor and often difficult to decipher. He wrote as he spoke, and one can almost detect the North Carolina/ Tennessee heritage in his "voice." When a word was so wildly misspelled as to be indiscernible we include a footnote to assist the reader. Punctuation was nearly nonexistent and we thought it appropriate to at least add periods where sentences were obviously intended to end. This was done strictly as a service to the reader and does not alter the content or the intent of the letters in any way.

Included in the surviving letters is the last letter written by Mary Elizabeth Paschal to her brother Newton before his capture at the Battle of Brice's Cross Roads. That letter, as well as a short emotional sentence Mary penned on the back of one of Tommy's letters which marked the one-year observance of Newton's death at Andersonville, has been reprinted in this volume.

Also printed herein are two letters Mary Elizabeth Paschal received from her cousin, Lt. Henry D. Freeman of Company D, 114th Illinois Regiment, including a dramatic letter informing Mary that Newton had been captured. The letter also describes Freeman's own capture and subsequent escape from a moving train transporting him to a Confederate prison.

Published for the first time in this second printing of *From Beardstown to Andersonville*, are three love letters written to Mary by Pvt. Thomas Cuppy of the 3rd Illinois Cavalry. Cuppy, who served as an orderly for Gen. Grenville Dodge, left Vicksburg on a sick boat in January 1863 and was never heard from again. Mary went on to wed a man twenty years her senior, a not uncommon occurrence in the 1860s, after so many young men were killed or rendered emotionally unstable by the Civil War.

Photograph by Donna Hess Cooper.

Mary Paschal Hobson's grave at the Chapin Cemetery in Chapin, Illinois. She is buried with her husband Jonathon Hobson and her son, Harry Newton Paschal, who was called Newton and named in honor of her brother. Ironically, Newton was the only one of Mary's six children who did not reach adulthood. Her other five children, including Clara Hobson Fulton, are buried in the Pacific Northwest.

Finally, this second printing includes descriptions of the movements and actions of the 114th Illinois; a more detailed description of the Battle of Brice's Cross Roads where Asa Newton Paschal was taken as a prisoner-of-war; and finally a description of Andersonville during Newton's imprisonment there in the horrible summer of 1864.

To the extent possible, footnotes have been added to identify the individuals mentioned and an asterisk at the end of a footnote denotes that further information is set forth in the Addendum. Brief biographical sketches of the various Union and Confederate leaders mentioned have also been included. Finally, an index is provided to help in the location of names, battles, towns, etc.

Part One

The Letters of

Pvt. Asa Newton Paschal,
Company A, 114th Illinois Infantry

Asa Newton Paschal.

Coleman Paschal was just 43 years old when he died during April of 1852 in Beardstown, Illinois. He left behind his wife Sarah "Sally" Street and eight children. His two oldest daughters, Margaret and Rachel, had both recently married, but the six other children, including four sons, were still minors and still at home. According to the 1850 census Coleman Paschal was the poorest farmer in his neighborhood. The total value of his real estate came to $400. All of his neighbors had land valued between $800 and $5000.

Fortunately for Sally the Paschal clan was a large one and her late husband's siblings were still alive and most of them were living in Illinois or across the border in Iowa. This included Sally's father-in-law, the venerable Isaiah Paschal, veteran of the War of 1812, who still worked as a blacksmith in the town of Virginia, just a few miles southeast of Beardstown.

Isaiah Paschal had arrived in Morgan County, Illinois, south of Cass County, with his wife Agnes Freeman and most of his children, in 1829. It was not the first time that Isaiah had demonstrated his pioneer spirit. Born in Warren County, North Carolina in 1781, Isaiah followed the western migration to Tennessee in 1806, either through the Cumberland Gap or on a new postal road that had opened the same year. With him were his wife and his three youngest children. The other ten would be born in Wilson County, Tennessee.

Paschal fought under the command of General Andrew Jackson as a private in the 1ˢᵗ Tennessee Volunteer Militia. He saw action against the Creek Indians and for his service he eventually received a land grant of 120 acres in Morgan County, Illinois. Paschal must have been a hardy soul. He died in 1877 at the age of 96, having outlived seven of his children and some of his grandchildren as well, including three of his son Coleman's children.

Whatever influence "Grand Pap" had on his grandsons is unknown, but it seems as if Asa Newton Paschal, the second son of Coleman, inherited his grandfather's adventurous spirit.

The children of Coleman Paschal and Sally Street were as follows:

1. Margaret Paschal was born in 1831, married Alexander Hutchinson and had two daughters, Jennie and Emma. She died in July of 1913 in Cass County, Illinois.

2. Rachel Paschal was born in April of 1833, married Nathaniel Peters on October 2, 1851, and had two sons, Jonnie and Eddie, both of whom died as teenagers. Rachel died in 1929 at age 96 and is buried in Diamond Grove Cemetery in Jacksonville, Illinois.

3. Joseph G. Paschal was born in 1835 and married Mary A. Crow on May 10, 1857. Mary was Joseph's cousin, the daughter of Ira and Rebecca (Street) Crow, Rebecca being the younger sister of his mother. Joseph died on May 3, 1869, and is buried in Beardstown City Cemetery in Cass County, Illinois.

4. Asa Newton Paschal was born in 1837. He died in the Confederate Prison at Andersonville, Georgia on the 20th of August 1864 and is buried there. He is remembered by tombstone # 6301. Unfortunately, his name is misspelled as J. M. Pashall.

5. Harriet Paschal was born in 1838 and married Hazen Skinner on December 5, 1860. She died in December of 1862 while Newton was away at war. Harriet and Hazen had a son Albert who was referred to in the letters as Birney.

6. William Henry Paschal, nicknamed " Old Grub", was born on May 4, 1840 in Hancock County, Illinois. He married first Emlin Dunn on December 24, 1863, and after her death on September 8,

1872, he married Emlin's sister Mary Ann Dunn on December 17, 1873. He was the father of seven children; lived his entire life on the family farm; died February 3, 1917, and is buried in Diamond Grove Cemetery in Jacksonville, Illinois. Brother William appears to be the son who accepts the responsibility of home, family and farm. William is 19 years old in July of 1859 when, as revealed by Newton's response, he writes to Newton suggesting he had better come home if "he is not a making money at the rate of two forty." William apparently also mentions a large melon patch and seems to suggest he could use some help from Newton, to which Newton replies he will let him know in his next letter. His "next" letter did not survive time so we do not know how soon he returned home to Illinois.

7. Mary "Mollie" Elizabeth Paschal was born on August 11, 1842, and married Jonathan Hobson on March 28, 1866. Mary and Jonathan raised a family of six children. Ironically, the only child who did not survive childhood was a son named in honor of Newton Pascal. Mary died on Thanksgiving Day, November 25, 1897, at Chapin, Illinois. Mary and Jonathan are buried with little Newton in Chapin Cemetery, Morgan County, Illinois. The rest of their children died in the Pacific Northwest and are survived by numerous descendants. Mary Elizabeth Paschal Hobson was the great-grandmother of Joseph E. Fulton, editor of this publication.

8. Samuel Thomas Paschal was the youngest sibling, having been born on April 23, 1848. At age 16, on March 3, 1865, Thomas enlisted in the 47th Illinois Infantry, Co. F, and served until January 21, 1866. His brothers often called him " Blake" while his sisters called him Tommy. He married Anna Wylder, the daughter of Jasper and Wilmuth (Jones) Wylder, on November 22, 1877. Sarah Lois, the only daughter of Thomas and Anna Paschal, married Wilbur Williams in Morgan County, and has descendants living in that area today. Thomas died on May 26, 1926, and is buried beside his wife Anna who preceded him in death on January 7, 1916, in Diamond Grove Cemetery, Jacksonville, Illinois.

Asa Newton Paschal was the one son who did wander extensively and spent very little of his adult life, short as it was, in Cass County. As soon as he was old enough to leave home he moved to Franklin, Lee

County, Iowa to live with his cousins and his dad's brother, Samuel Paschal. Samuel Paschal was married to Hannah Street, a younger sister of Newton's mother. Samuel and Hannah were also the parents of eight children including Mary Ella Paschal, great-great grandmother of Donna Cooper, an Iowan genealogist who contributed the extensive biographical addendum found at the end of this book.

Five of Samuel and Hannah's children were still at home during the period of Newton's stay. Newton attended a small school in nearby Clay Grove where the teacher was a 30 year-old man from Pennsylvania named A. H. Ringland.

Newton's first letter is dated about six years after the death of his father, on January 20, 1858, and is written from Clay Grove. Despite Newton's apparent desire to investigate horizons outside his home state, his heart was always at home, and he wrote the first letter published herein to let his family know how he was doing.

Clay Grove[1], Iowa, January 30, 1858

My Dear Sister [Harriet]: I now imbrace the present opportunity of writing you a few lines to let you know that I am well and all the relations as far as I know. Well, Harriet, I received your letters them that you wrote to me. I got one last week that related to me the death of Mrs. Tredway and the one before the death of Mr. Haywood but the last letter I received from you dated January the 21 brought to me the sad news of an other of my acquaintances which gave me much pain but I hope that she was prepared for a better land. My dear sister, thare is no telling how soon that we shall have to die like those friends of ours sooner or later, so lets us try and be prepared to meet our heavenly father, so I will say no more on that most important subject at the present. Well, Harriet, I will try to write some thing about how I am getting along now. I am a going to school and I think that I am a learning very fast. I am a going

---

1   Clay Grove was a small town in Lee County, Iowa. The town no longer exists.

to a man by the name of Ringland. He is a firstrait teacher and learns the schollars very fast. I am a boarding at Uncle Samuels². The school will be out by the first of March and I aspect to come back home some time in March or the first of April and I hope that you will not think the time long for I think that I am a doing as well as if I wear at home. I have enjoyed my self very well ever since I left home. I havent had a ounce of sickness since I started and have not seen many that was sick. Well, Harriet, I will quit for this time for I dont feel much like writing on the account of the news that you sent me, the death of one that I near shall forget. So no more at present. Write as soon as you receive this. I am your affectionate brother until death, A. N. Paschal to Miss H. E. Paschal

The only other pre-Civil War letter that survives from Newton finds the young man some 300 miles west of his Uncle Samuel's home in Lee County, Iowa. In 1859 Newton moved to the Nebraska Territory and found work at a sawmill in the town of Peru. Peru had been established in September of 1857 but it and much of Nemaha County, situated along the Missouri River in the far southeast corner of Nebraska, was settled by the time young Newton arrived. Because fur traders, gold seekers and pioneers took advantage of the transportation on the Missouri River, the towns along the river were the first to be settled in the Nebraska Territory. Peru, Nebraska is located on a bluff above the Missouri River. Newton mentions "800 grown persons and children to numerous to mention" at the July 4, 1859, Independence Day celebration in Peru. But Peru never became a very big town. Its present day population is less than 600.

At the time of Newton's arrival Peru and other towns in Nemaha County were buzzing with abolitionists. Many of John Brown's followers lived in the area. Ironically, Newton made it clear in a letter written four years later that he did not think too highly of abolitionists. (See letter of January 17, 1863)

Newton had traveled to the Nebraska Territory accompanied by

2   Samuel Paschal, his father's brother.

friends and cousins from Illinois seeking the newly discovered gold of Colorado. As the following letter reveals he passed up the initial opportunity to continue the venture to the gold country of Pike's Peak, Colorado, but does not completely rule out the journey if his friends will write and tell him that "times are good . . . and there is no danger of starving to death . . ."

Known as the "Fifty-Niners" and the "Pike Peakers", nearly 100,000 prospectors rushed to Colorado after gold was discovered on Pike's Peak the previous year. Because of the extreme weather in the Rocky Mountains many prospectors did not reach their goal, but the rush helped create many new cities in the area, including Denver, Colorado.

Nebraska became the 37th state on March 1, 1867. When Newton lived there the entire population of the territory was less than 28,000.

Peru, Nebraska, April 30, 1859

Dear Sister [Mary]: It is with pleasure I sit down to write a few lines to let you know that I am well and hope these few lines will arrive safe and find you all the same. I am still in Nebraska. I have been at work in a saw mill for the last month at eighteen dollars per month and expect to work until the first of July it has been about two months since I have gotten any letters from any of you and I fear thare is something the matter or else you did not know where to write to. Times out here are better than they have been all winter. The weather is fine and things are a growing nice. Thare is plenty of grass for the stock, produce has come up to a good price, wheat is 12.5 cts per bushel, corn is 50, oats 50, Potatoes 50, bacon 15 cts per lb and all other produce according. John Davis, James Anderson & several others left here for Pikes Peke this day two weeks ago. They wanted me to go with them but I considered that I would not go until I found out more about the place. Thare is several that promised to write to me as soon as they get thare. If times are good out thare & no danger of starving to death perhaps I may go out thare this fall. I would like to know if Mr Hutchason[3] has moved to Kansas or not and if they have how long cince. And I would like to know how the wheat looks since warm weather set in and wheather Nig[3] is alive yet. Selie and Alfis[4] wishes to be remembered by all of you. James and Levi[5] sends there best respects to you and Harriet[6]. Tell Nathaniel Peters and Rachel[7] that I have not forgotten them and I would like for them to write to me. If thare is any pretty girls out thare that wants to marry just tell tham that I am single yet. I must bring my letter to a close. Write soon. From your brother, A.N. Paschal, to Miss Mary E. Paschal. PS. Direct your letters to Peru, Nemaha Co., N. T.

Peru, Nebraska, July 6, 1859

Dear Brother [William]: I now sit down to write you a few words to let you know that I am well and all the relations as far as I no. I received your kind letter dated June the 5th and was glad to hear from you all. I have nothing of much importance to write. Thare was a very large cellebration at Peru on the fourth which went off just about rite. Thare was over eight hundred grown persons and children to numerous to mention. You wrote to me if I was not a making money at the rate of two forty that I had better start for home. Well, William, I ant a doing any big things for times has been so hard ever since I have been out hear, but times is a getting better by degrees. Crops of all kinds looks well out here. I am a going up to

---

3   It is unknown to whom Newton is referring. Since his inquiry seems rather off-hand, perhaps Nig was a horse or pet.

4   Probably Alfie Brown to whom Newton refers in a later letter. Selie may have been his wife.

5   James Brown and Levi Brown were close neighbors of the Paschal family. (*Brown)

6   Harriet, his sister.

7   Sister Rachel and her husband, Nathaniel Peters.

Plattsmouth[8] on a visit. I am a going to start in the morning so you may direct your next letter to Plattsmouth Cass Co. N.T. I will write to you a gain shortly after I get up thare. I would like to see you all very well but I cant promice you at the present time wheather I will come home this sumer or not. I like to live out here better for it is healthiyer and the people are not troubled with the big head. They are all sociable and peacible and live at home. I have enjoyed myself very well ever since I have been out here. I escorted one of the fair sex home from the selebration, thats so. You said that you had a fine mellon patch. I will let you know wheather I will be thare to help you with them or not in my next letter. You must excuse this short letter for I have written it in haste. So no more at present. Yours in respect, A.N. Paschal

Newton Paschal did not return to Illinois that summer, nor did he return the following year. He did not stay in Nemaha County, Nebraska, nor return to his uncle's farm in Iowa. In fact, Newton Paschal is nowhere to be found in the 1860 federal census. There is a Newton Paschal in that census, but he is Asa Newton's distant cousin, a young physician from Tennessee living in Missouri.

So where was Asa Newton Paschal? Perhaps he did as he suggested he might do in the fall of 1859 and headed off to Pike's Peak to join his friends in search of gold. That might explain how he managed to avoid the census takers. All we know for sure is that he did return to Cass County, Illinois sometime between 1860 and 1862. The Civil War broke out in April 1861 but Newton did not immediately answer the call. However, when it was announced in July 1862 that a new regiment would be formed and it would include the boys of Cass County, Newton joined many of his friends and volunteered.

The 114th Illinois would come to be known as the "Sangamon Regi-

---

8   Plattsmouth, Nebraska is approximately 40 miles north of Peru, with a present-day population of about 7,000. Located at the confluence of the Platte and Missouri Rivers, it was founded by fur traders. Older than the state itself, the town was incorporated on March 15, 1855.

ment" because six of the ten companies were comprised of men from that Illinois County. Companies F and K came from Menard County and companies A and D were from Cass County. The commanding officer of the 114th was Colonel James W. Judy. The volunteers were to report to Camp Butler at Clear Lake near Springfield, the hometown of President Abraham Lincoln. Among the men from Cass County reporting with Newton were his brother Joseph and his cousins William Crow and Henry Freeman. Joseph didn't make it. According to Newton his brother got very sick and went back home.

Cousin William Crow made it a bit longer. Nevertheless, he deserted in June of 1863 during the Vicksburg campaign. Cousin Henry Freeman rose to the rank of First Lieutenant. His dramatic escape from a train that was taking him to a prisoner-of-war camp can be found in this book. Along with Newton and his friends from Cass County, thousands of other men reported to Camp Butler to form six new regiments during the summer of 1862. They came by horse, on foot, down the Sangamon River or by the Great Western Railroad.

According to John L. Satterlee in his book *The Journal & The 114th, 1861 to 1865*, the volunteers were issued a uniform "consisting of a long dark blue coat reaching down to the knees….trousers were sky blue wool, held up with braces." The men also received a kepi, or forage cap, and some of their equipment included "woolen blankets, knapsacks, haversacks and canteens, cartridge box and cap box." Most of the men had a single-shot, muzzle-loading rifle. Infantry units like the 114th would also have bayonets for their rifles. The bullet was the "minie" ball, an elongated piece of lead with a pointed head and hollow base that was much more accurate and more deadly than the old musket balls used in previous American wars.

Four letters survive from Newton's two months of training and waiting at Camp Butler. The first was written on September 15, 1862, just three days before the 114th Illinois was mustered into service.

Camp Butler, Illinois, September 15, 1862

Dear Sister: It is with pleasure I take my pen in hand to answer your kind letter of the thirteenth. I was glad to here

*you are all well or a mending. I am well and all of my acquan-
tences. William Crow[9] has been under the weather but has
got better. Brother Joseph left here for home last Saturday. He
was very sick. He was taken sick with a chill. I fear it is a going
to go hard with him. I am very anxious to hear from him. I
wish that I had of a come home with him although he came
home with a man that would take as good care of him as I
could my self I have no doubt. I hope he got home safe. The
Virginia[10] Company is in our regiment. They appear to enjoy
themselves very well but some of them are a getting home sick.
Thomas Brown[11] is a writing a letter on a clap board with me
to his mother. We were all mustered in a few days a go except
one company and when it came to be mustered it fell short
11 men of being a full company and of corse could not be
mustered and came very near breaking up the Regiment but
as it hapend some of the companies had a surplus of men and
they have volentered to fill up the deficiency in said Company
so we will all have to be mustered in a gain. We cannot draw
our bounty untill we are mustered or get a furlow to come
home. Our Company drawed its uniform this morning. It is
fine looking company you had better believe. Captain M[12] was
elected major and we elected John Johnson in his place. He
makes a very good Captain so you can send your letters in care
of Capt Johnson. I must bring my letter to a close. You must
excuse bad writing for I burnt my finger the other day. Write
soon, so no more at present. A. N. Paschal*

---

9   William F. Crow (114th Ill., Co. A) was a brother of Mary A. Crow, wife of
     Newton's oldest brother Joseph. William and his sister were also a first cousins to
     Newton and his siblings because their mother, Rebecca Street Crow, was the sister
     of Sally Street Paschal.

10   Virginia, Illinois is a small town in Cass County. It is the present day county seat of
     Cass County.

11   Thomas H. Brown (114th Ill, Co. D). (*Brown)

12   Major Joseph Milton McLane. (*McLane)

Camp Butler, October 2, 1862

Dear Sister: It is with pleasure I take my pen in hand to let you know that I am well at present and hope this will find you all enjoying the same blessing. It was my intention to come home before I left this Camp but it appears that I cannot as we are to leave here pretty soon. I wanted to come down with William but I could not get off. Our Captain letts the married men go home but the single men has to stay at camp. Wm Crow has gone home but he would not of got to go iff he had not got sick. I dont expect to come home before we leave here. We will leave here about next Tuesday to some unknown point and I dont care where just so we get [going] and can be of some benefit to our Country. Their is to be a regiment leave here every other day until this camp is entirely empty. All of the boys are in good spirits and rejoice to think that they are to leave here so soon. We have got a splendid lot of guns and good equipage, the best in camp. Our uniform is very nice. You had better believe that we look nice when we all march out in perade. I think that we will give a good account of our selves when we get down in Dixie. Tell my friends that I think that they might write to me once and a while just for an accomodation if nothing else for it would oblige me very much. I will endeavor to answer all the letters that I get. I wrote a letter to Mr. N. Peters a few days ago but have no answer yet but I recon it is hardly time yet to get an answer. We have several visitors from Cass County. I hear from home every few days but when we get away from here news from home will be scattering and far between but be it as it may I shall try and feel content. We had a very hard rain up here last evening accompanied by considerable hail about the size of plums and considerable wind. We expect to get the letter of our Company this afternoon. It was the entention to drill for it but we have not time to drill for the letter so it will be left for the Colonel to decide. All of the companies wants letter A and I cant tell who will get it yet but

I will let you know in my next letter. Write as soon as you get this letter. So no more at present. A. N. Paschal

The following letter, written to his youngest brother Tommy, is one of the most endearing in the collection. Newton, who is eleven years older than Tommy, asks his little brother to keep cattle from running over mother, "give the geese and ducks fitts" and "go to school in the winter… and not be hugging and kissing the girls all the time."

Camp Butler, Illinois, October 5, 1862

Well, Thomas[13], I will send you a few lines to let you know that I have not forgotten you. I expect you are the best man left on the farm. I want you to tan old Grub[14] once and a while if he getts to running about of knights and leves you all the work to do. I want you to get plenty of ammunition and give the geese and ducks fitts. I want you to make them think that I had not left their at all or if I had that I had left a brother that could shoot as good as I could and perhaps a little better. Kill all of the stray dogs that bothers you and make things come to center all around that neighborhood. Dont let your mother be run over by any one or anyones stock. Just knock things end ways iff they dont come to center. I want you to be a good boy and not work to hard and go to school this winter if you get any time. I want you to study your books and not be huging and kissing the girls all the time. But perhaps you will not thank me for my advice but if you do not, just do as you please. I am easy sooted any way for I expect your head is about as long as mine any way. Tell Mary[15] that I got that testiment that she

---

13 Samuel Thomas Paschal was 14 years of age when he received this letter from his big brother.

14 Old Grub was a nickname Newton used for his brother William Paschal.

15 Newton's sister Mary Elizabeth Paschal.

sent me by Crow. I would like to see you all very well but as I cannot I will trouble you once and a while with a letter. I do not expect to write very often unless pretty good oppertunities for it is almost imposible to write when we are a traveling a bout from place to place. I want all of my letters answered promptly and then I will feel more like visiting. Iff any of the girls asks you any thing about me just tell them that I am all rite and in good health and good sperits and good bisiness. Tell them that I dont expect to quit the army until peace is declared through out the Union if I should have no bad luck. Tell the neighbors that we are Company A and march on the right of the Regiment and all the rest has to follow us. I believe I will bring my letter to a close by saying Hurraw for the Union. I cannot tell you where to direct your letters to at present but as soon as I get to our next camping place I will write again. Yours with respect, Asa N. Paschal

Camp Butler, October 23, 1862

Dear Sister [Mary]: It is with pleasure I take my pen in hand to answer your letter which came to hand yesterday. It found me well and this leves me the same. I was glad to hear from you all and that you were getting along all rite and was done with the measels. I think I just left home in time or I would have got them to for it appears that their was enough of them for the whole family. The health of the people up here is jenerly good. All the Regiments that are encamped here marched to Springfield and back yesterday and had a fine time you had better believe. We had our napsacs, canteenes and one days provisions. We started from camp at ten oclock in the morning and got back just at dark. We marched about fifteen miles in all. Some of the boys got very tyred of their trip but it was fun for me. The road was dry and nice. Their was a string of men about a mile long four in a breast. Our

*regiment done very well in the perade ground. They moved
very nice. Not changing the subject it begins to look kinder
winterish this morning and feels the same way. I thought for a
while that we would get down south before cold weather but I
dont here much talk of leveing here lately. Their are more talk
of wintering here at the present time but I dont bother my self
much about any thing. It would not make two cents difference
to leve or stay. The Major says that I take things just about as
cool as any one in camp. I want you to tell Grub that I never
got his letter that he wrote to me and would like him to write
again but I expect that he is very busy this fall and having the
measeles to boot that he has not much time to write. I expect
you think that I feel very lonesome up here since Joe[16] and
Bill Crow left but if you do you are mistaken for I feel better
satisfied that they are at home when I take their health in
consideration for this is a very poor place for any body that
is sick or has poor health. It is a great deal better for them
to be at home where they can be properly tended to and get
such food as is suitable for any one sick to eat & soon. Mr.
Lindsley[17] has been complaining considerable since he came
back from home but is still able to knock about the camp. Tell
Mother that it is not because I have forgotten her that I do not
write. Tell her that when I write to you I mean it for the whole
family. Tell her that I thought it was a considerable task for
her to write and I thought that I would make you do all the
writing. Tell Thomas that I will excuse him for not answering
my letter for I did not expect an answer any way. I believe
that I have written all that I can get on this paper decently.
Give my love to all enquiring friends. So no more at present.
Yours with respect, A. N. Paschal*

---

16   Joseph Paschal, Newton's brother.

17   Erastus Darwin Lindsley (114th Ill, Co. D). (*Lindsley)

Camp Butler, Illinois, October 30, 1862

*Dear Sister [Mary]: It is with pleasure I take my pen in hand
to write you a few lines to let you know that I am well and
hope this will find you all the same. I wrote William a letter
yesterday and sent it by Darwin Lindsley. He left here this
morning. He has been sick since he came up here. I do not
believe that souldiers life agrees with him very well. John
Haywood, Thomas [K]night, Mrs. Harris and others[18] are
here to day. They will leve here for home this evening and I
expect that I will send this letter by some one of them. I cant
think of any thing to write that will amuse you. Urban's wife[19]
is up here. She came up yesterday evening. She says that the
relations are all well up about Virginia. I think about comeing
down home on the election day but cannot tell for certain
yet whether I will or not. I will know as soon as our Colonel
gets back. He is gone home but will be back tomorrow. This
is very fine weather for camping. I wish that I could be down
there in the Sangamon botom a gathering pecans. Wm wrote
to me that the water was so high that he could not get in the
timber to get any wood or any thing else and I think that must
be very provoking indeed. I expect that you will have to cook
this winter without any fire and that will be a very hard task
until you get ust to it. I expect that Blake and Grub is very
busy this fine weather a diging potatoes or gathering corn or
doing something else. I wish this war would come to a close
for it looks very bad to see so many men a doing nothing when
they could be at home at work and taking care of their families
but I do not see any more signes of it coming to a close than
their was six months ago or hardly as mutch. It looks like the
officers do not care how long it lasts for they are a doing well*

---

18   Visiting for the day were members of the family of Joseph Haywood, Newton's
     close friend who was also in the 114th Regiment, John Haywood and his wife,
     Caroline Harris Haywood; Thomas and Emeline (Haywood) Knight and Caroline
     Harris Haywood's mother. (*Haywood)

19   Newton's cousin, Mary Catherine Paschal, married to Urban Pedigo. (*Pedigo)

enough as long as Uncle Sam is worth any thing. I believe
that they had all [rather] talk poytics than fight or at least it
appears to me that way. It looks to me like the north might
get along a little faster if she would use some of the Regiment
at this camp. The Regiment is very well drilled and getting
tired of staying here. They are very anxious to go south and
try their luck on the rebels and would go if they could get their
pay. Their was one regiment payed a day or two ago and will
leve in a few days. It was a German Regiment. I believe it only
has three Americans in it. I will bring this letter to a close by
saying write soon. Yours truly, A. N. Paschal

After weeks of drilling and anticipation the men of the 114th received their first marching orders and left Camp Butler on Saturday morning, November 8, 1862. The destination was Memphis, Tennessee, which had been captured by Union forces in a quick battle on June 6th of that year. Memphis was a staging area for Union troops as they sought to gain control of the entire Mississippi River, a critical supply and transportation route for the Confederate Army.

A newspaper reporter for The Illinois Journal who went by the penname of "The Observer," carefully recorded much of these first movements by the 114th after they left the relatively safe confines of Camp Butler.

The men of the 114th took a train from Camp Butler to Alton, Illinois, a small town on the confluence of the Mississippi and Missouri Rivers. At Alton the men boarded boats for Columbus, Kentucky passing St. Louis en route. Mallory described the boat ride as an "unpleasant passage" because the boat's captain was " a drunken brute; a rabid enemy of the administration."

The 114th stopped briefly in Cairo, Illinois on the confluence of the Mississippi and Ohio Rivers at the southernmost point in Illinois. This was one of the most strategic points in the western front of the Civil War. With General U.S. Grant in command, Cairo was the first point of troop concentration for the Mississippi River campaign. Furthermore, virtually all correspondence between troops and their families went through Cairo. Despite tens of thousands of Union troops passing through the town, Cairo itself had only about 2,000 citizens. Today it has about 4,000 and remains most famous for its role in the Civil War.

The next stop for the 114th was Columbus, Kentucky, where the men saw numerous slaves wandering around in an otherwise abandoned town. The slaves sought the protection of the Union troops in anticipation of reports that President Lincoln was about to emancipate them. Kentucky never seceded from the Union, but it was full of Confederate sympathizers and Confederate guerrilla bands were very active in the border state.

Newton tells his sister Mary in a letter written shortly after his arrival in Memphis that he saw battlefields and forts from the boat. He saw Belmont, Arkansas, across the river from Columbus, where Grant fought his first battle, a losing one, against Confederate forces. He also saw Ft. Pillow, Ft. Wright and Island No. 10 where Confederate forces surrendered one of their most critical Mississippi River strongholds on April 7, 1862.

The 114th landed in Memphis on Saturday, November 15th and remained there on picket duty, awaiting further orders for less than two weeks. The following two dramatic letters, written on November 21st and 22nd, reveal some of Newton's thoughts and actions while camping in Memphis.

Camp Near Memphis, Tennesse, November 21, 1862

Dear Sister [Mary]: It is with pleasure I take pen in hand to write and let you know that I am well at present and hope this will find you all the same. I have had the yellow jandus but have got well of them. They did not hurt me mutch, only spoilt my apetite for about a week. That was all the injury that I could see that they done me. We are encamped in a very nice place. The weather is fine down here in Dixie. It is not cold enough to freeze any yet. Their has been considerable frost. The leaves are mostly killed with the frost but not entirely. I like this Country very well. I think it would be a

very nice place to live if the sesesh[20] wasent so thick. I do not
know how long we will stay at this place but I do not expect
we will stay mutch longer as their is no sesesh troops near at
the present time. Their is a large amount of union troops at
this place and I think it is their entention to make a move in a
few days for some point below here. I think our move next will
be down in Mississippi and if we go down there we will be apt
to have some fun with the rebels for they are said to be down
their pretty thick. Old Price[21] is near Holow Springs[22] and is
likely to give us a battle at Holow Springs or between there
and Vixberge. Vixberge is still in the hands of the rebels and is
considered one of their strongest fortifications that they hold at
the present time. I saw the battlefield of Bellmont, also Island
No. 10[23] and several other forts as I came down the river. I
expected to get some pay when I was in service three months
but I have found out it is a mistake about getting payed
regularly. I dont believe that Old Uncle is very full of money
these days. I expect that I will have to quit writing letters
pretty soon on account of postage stamps being so hard to get.
I cant get stamps without gold or silver and that is as scarse as
hens teeth down here and if any of my friends wants to here
from me very often they must send me a stamp occasionaly
thats so, but not because I am to near straped or to stingy to
buy. You need not fear of me a starving or getting to poor to
buy stamps to send letters to my friends as long as they can be

---

20 "Secessionists" or "Secessioners" were terms used to refer to members of the
    Southern Confederate States who had seceded from the Union. Newton uses a
    shortened version of those terms.

21 Major General Sterling Price, CSA (1809-1867) was commanding the Corps of
    the Confederate Army of the West at the time of this letter. He suffered defeats at
    Helena and Little Rock, Arkansas, and Westport, Missouri. Subject to a Confeder-
    ate inquiry toward the end of the war, Price moved to Mexico after the Union was
    restored.

22 Holly Springs, Mississippi was a supply post for the Union troops.

23 Island No. 10 near New Madrid, Missouri on the Mississippi River and was pro-
    tected on both sides by Confederate batteries until its capture by Union gunboats
    under the command of A. H. Foote.

*got on reasonable terms and at the present time they cannot.
Souldering is a getting to be an old thing to me and I don't care
mutch how things goes it is all the same to me, so I get plenty
to eat and wear. We get plenty of beef, pork, beans, sugar,
coffee, rice, peral hominy & so forth. This is a list of our grub.*

November 22, 1862 (this continues the above letter)

*That other sheet was rather small so I thought that I would
continue on an other sheet. I will mention something about
the enhabitance of this Country. It is mostly enhabited by
Negroes and Widoes, white men are very scarce. The most
of the men have taken the oath. The citizens about here say
the war will close between this and the first of May but they
think it will end in their favor and still they agree that our
army is superior to theirs and they say that two or three
more battles will tell the tale. Their was a fire in Memphis
last knight. Their was five houses burned, damage estimated
at fifty thousand dollars. Their are fire in this City almost
every knight. Ses esh property suffers down here in spite of
the officers. The officers still go on the plan of guarding sesesh
property but the souldiers do not. The souldiers will steel out
at camp of the knight and set fire to a building and then get
back to Camp as soon as possable and when the alarm is
raised that their is a fire no body knows any thing about it.
That is the way things goes down here. If all of the men was
like me we would clear out them thats so, for I say as long as
they guard sesesh property it is no use to fight them at all. The
Commander at this place allows sesesh to come in town ever
day and do their trading. The rebels brings in cotten and sells
it and takes out salt flower and provisions of all kinds but not
in very large [amounts, but] every little is a help to them. We
are not allowed to cross their lines without being shot at and
they can pass through our lines without being molested. Such*

work as this wont do much longer for the soldiers will not
stand it if the govenrnent dont pass better laws pretty soon.
All of the souldiers will rebell and let the goverment go to the
dickence. This war is a money making scam for the officers.
I heard one wish that it would last a year longer and I heard
a private say if it did he would not see it end, so if the officers
wants it to go on they had better keep their mouths shut, thats
my opinion of things. The Colonel says that his men shant
guard rebel propperty if he can help it and the major says the
same. I think that our regimental officers are all rite and I
know the men is thats so. Give my love to all. So no more at
present. Yours with respect, A. N. Paschall Direct your letters
to Memphis Tennisee Co A. 114 Reg Ills Vollenteers.

On Tuesday, November 25th the 114th left Memphis and headed to Mississippi. Confederate troops or rebel sympathizers tried to make the going tough by burning the bridges five miles south of Memphis. They had to be rebuilt and the regiment only made another five miles before setting camp near Horn Lake, Mississippi. On the 26th they marched another 12 miles south to Coldwater. According to W.A. Mallory the Union troops took possession of an abandoned plantation and many were sleeping on piles of cotton in a warehouse when the ever-surreptitious rebels set the warehouse on fire. Mallory called the spectacle "sublime." He explained to the Journal:

"Several thousand pounds of cotton was on fire, and the light sheets lifted by the wind, soared up and out in every direction, filling the air with flame and literally covering the ground with sparks and flakes of fire." The men in the warehouse escaped with their lives but not much of their gear. According to Mallory only one soldier died during the ensuing chaos of that memorable night when a tree fell on him.

Over the next couple of days the 114th traveled northwest along the Coldwater River, foraging freely from mostly abandoned farms, and spent the night of the 28th on Pigeon Roost Creek near Holly Springs, Mississippi. On the 30th the men could hear cannon fire to the south. It came from advance troops of General Grant along the Tallahatchie

River. However, the 114th was not ordered to join in the skirmish. Instead they marched west to the town of Chulahoma where they were informed that the rebels had dug in along the Tallahatchie west of Oxford to stop the Union advance. Some Union troops were sent to investigate but found no rebels. On December 2nd the 114th camped eight miles north of Oxford, Mississippi.

There the 114th and other Union regiments remained encamped for nearly three weeks. No doubt they engaged in lively debates over Lincoln's Emancipation Proclamation, set to take effect on January 1st. In a letter written by William Mallory on January 14th from Jackson, Tennessee, the 114th was "firmly united" in support of the proclamation. However, Newton asserts in a letter dated January 17th that "Lincoln's Proclamation does not suit the soldiers as well as it was anticipated it would."

On December 20th, Major General Earl Van Dorn, CSA and his cavalry were wreaking havoc on Union supply lines in Holly Springs and a few days later General Nathan Bedford Forrest, CSA destroyed the railway leading into Jackson, Tennessee. On Christmas Day, 1862, the 114th was ordered north to Jackson. They arrived after two weeks of hard marching on January 8th, 1863. Somewhere along the way Newton manages to meet pretty girls and claims that he, "Sparkled one all knight…and you better believe I gave her a good hugging."

Newton expressed frustration that several letters written during his weeks in Mississippi never made it to Beardstown. The editor of this collection shares that frustration. We will likely never know how many more letters were written by Newton during his service in the 114th, and letters that were lost forever on trains, steamboats or precarious mail routes used during the Civil War.

Jackson, Tennesee, January 9, 1863

Dear Brother [William]: I will try to write you a few lines this morning to let you know that I am well and hope this will find you all the same as I havent heard from home cinse I left and have written several times. I have almost come to the conclusion that it is no use to write until I get to the Mississippi river

or some other mail rout to the north. The mail to this regiment
has been twist once at Holow Springs and on a steem boat on
the Miss river and the devil knows where the rest of it has gone.
We have been on the march for two weeks after old Forests[24]
cavelry but they kept up such running that we could not get
a shot at them but we run them on to old Sullivan[25] and he
gave them fits. Took five hundred prisenors, eight peaces of
artillery and a no. of small arms. This is the way they get payed
back for burning our railroad bridges and putting us to so
much trouble. They burnt up ten days grub for Grants[26] whole
army at Holow Springs and I guess they thought that they
would starve us out but we was to sharp for them. We went to
subsisting on the sitizens and you had better believe we make
the chickens and hogs cattle turkeys and every thing else suffer
that is good to eat. Rosencrant[27] and Brag[28] has run to gather
lately and have had a hi old fight but I havent heard the partic-
ulars yet. Vicsberg is also atacked and reported taken but not
confirmed. I expect that you think that I have been in a battle
or two before this time but I havent seen a rebel with arms yet.
I have traveled over considerable of the suny south and have
enjoyed my self well with the trip so far. We drew a new lot
of clothes this morning but we havent got a pull at the green

---

24 Brig. Gen. Nathan Bedford Forrest, CSA, (1821-1877), native of Tennessee, was commanding the cavalry brigade of the Confederate Army of Tennessee at the time of this letter.

25 Brig. Gen. Jeremiah Cutler Sullivan (1830-1890), native of Indiana, was commanding District of Jackson, Left Wing, 16th Corps, Army of the Tennessee, at the time of this letter.

26 Maj. Gen. Ulysses Simpson Grant (1822-1885), native of Ohio, was commanding the U. S. Army of the Tennessee at the time of this letter. He became Commander-in-Chief of the United States Army on March 12, 1864, and 18th President of the United States in 1869.

27 Brig. Gen. William Starke Rosecrans (1819-1898) was a native of Ohio. Ironically, he served his final day as Commander of the 14th Corps, Army of the Cumberland, and became strictly the Commander of the Army of the Cumberland (formerly Army of the Ohio) on January 9, 1863, the day this letter was written.

28 Gen. Braxton Bragg, CSA, (1817-1876), native of North Carolina, was Confederate Commander of the Army of Tennessee at the time of this letter.

backs yet. I dont believe that their is a dollar in our Company at the present time. I have got fifteen cents yet and I am a going to keep it for seed for I dont know when I will get any more. I expect that we will be leveing in a day or two and that suits me very well for I had rather be a traviling than staying still. Our Regiment is very healthy at present and I guess it is because we live like hogs. We havent got any tents and get wet every time it rains and that keeps us clean and healthy. Our tents are at Memphis yet. We sent the Chaplin[29] after them but we havent heard from him since and I guess we wont as long as we keep traveling. None of the boys that we left at home when we started from Camp Butler that belong to our Co has got with us but Luther Main[30] yet. I dont know how match longer this war will last but I do not expect it will end very soon. It tickles me when I think of how the people ust to talk about starving the rebels out. They were greatly mistaken for their is plenty of corn wheat hogs cattle sheep and other things down hear to last both armies twelve months yet if their wasnt any thing raised this coming season. I think that the only way to get them out is to whip them out. Some of the boys is making great calculations on going home this spring but I am a feard that they will slip up on that idea and furlows are played out entirely and the parolling buisness has come to an end and the only way to get home is to desert or wait until the war closes. Thomas Brown got a letter from Alf about two weeks ago stating his Brother Levi[31] was dead. He died with the brain fever and was taken home and buried at Peru. I saw Steven[32] the other day and he is as develish as ever. I saw Let Beals[33]. He has been sick and looks kinder slim but he is emproving fast. Their is lots of pretty

---

29   Chaplin of the 114th was Caleb P. Baldwin.

30   Luther Maine (114th Ill, Co. A). (*Maine)

31   Levi N. Brown (Co. C, 2nd Nebraska Cavalry) is buried in Mount Vernon Cemetery, Peru, Nebraska. (*Brown)

32   Probably Stephen Brown, Thomas' brother.

33   Lester Beals, son of Alvord and Charlotte Beals, neighbors of the Paschal family.

girls down here in Dixie and they all want to marry the worst kind. The most of them are very anxious for the war to come to a close. They take great fancy to the northern men. I sparkled one all knight about a week ago and you had better believe I gave her a good huging. Their are a great many Union folks in this state. I think it will come back in the Union before long but Mississippi is gone without doubt. I never saw a union man down there all the time I was in the state. Tennesee is as pretty country as I ever saw. Their is the best timber I ever saw in my life. The land is tollerable good in places. The corn averages about 30 bushels to the acre and wheat grows very well in this part of the state. Well I must tell you how we enjoyed Christmas and New Years. On Christmas Eve we laid in a plenty of chicken and turkeys and we had a splendid supper and breakfast and marched all day and on New Years day we done the same only we had a barel of whiskey aded to the Regiment and it made some of the boys feel very funny. One or two got to feeling upwards for the ground and thats the way New Years went. P.S. Write soon and give me the news. Direct your letters to via Cairo, Ills. Yours truly, A.N.Paschal

Jackson, Tennesee, January 17, 1863

Dear Sister [Mary]: It is with pleasure I take my pen in hand to answer your kind letter dated Dec the 18. I was very glad to hear from you all. I also received a letter from William. He stated that sister Hattie was sick and I have been considerable uneasy ever since.[34] I had ought to write to Grub but your letter was written first and I expect your all a looking for an answer before this time. As it is quite a task to write a letter I send this to the both of you. The weather down here is very disagreeable at present. Their is about six inches of snow

---

34 Hattie died in late December of 1862 but Newton had not yet received the news.

on the ground, pretty cool to boot but we are a getting along
tollerable well. We have got our tents again and encamped
where their is plenty of wood. We have been at this place
for over a week and their is no talk of our leaving here any
ways soon. I havent any news of any emportance to write at
present. News is very scarce out here concerning the war. At
present the souldiers appears to be a thinking more about
the way the free states are doing than the South are acting.
Their is considrable excitement in camp at the present time
about different reselutions that has been discussed in the free
states. Some regiments has stacked their arms and swore that
they would fight no more under the present circumstances.
It is almost imposable for us to get a newspaper at present.
It appears that they want to keep the souldiers in ignorance
as much as posable. It appears that the army is on a stand
whether to fight or not. Lincoln's Proclamation[35] does not suit
the souldiers as well as it was anticipated it would. This thing
of freeing negroes doesnt set well amongst the souldiers and
the souldiers has almost come to the conclusion that that is all
that keeps up this war. They think that the President and his
cabinet will not hear to any thing else, only the emancipation
of all the slaves. For my part I believe that this war could be
settled honerably to both north and south if it wasnt for the
pride of the two contending parties. It looks like we have quit
fighting for the Union and went to fighting for the negro. Some
of our abolitionist[36] friends say if they can't free the negro
that they will never return to the North and they all preach
up that it is the only thing that will ever make the northern
states wealthy. I wish that every abolitionist would turn two
shades blacker than any negro in the south and if the negroes

35 President Lincoln signed the Emancipation Proclamation on January 1, 1863,
    potentially abolishing slavery.

36 The abolitionists belonged to a movement professing the total abolition of slave
    trade. In the United States, this movement was led chiefly by William Lloyd Gar-
    rison, Theodore Dwight Weld and Frederick Douglas.

is ever set free in the free states, I never want to lay down my old musket until I chase them out. The Southern States swears that they will not employ free negroes and if the North frees them, they will have to take them out of the southern states and do the best they can with them for they will never submit to live with free negroes. And I am of the opinion that once our goverment gets them free that it will not be able to send them out of the country and of course it will have to keep them and this is just what the abolitionest glories in. And under such circumstances we may not look for peace any ways soon. But let this world wag as it will, I will be gay and happy still. So no more at present. Write soon and give me the news. Yours with Respect, AN Paschal. Direct your letters to the 114th Ills Vol Reg, Co A, via Cairo, Ills. PS. The reason why I have my letters directed to Cairo is that that is the General Distributing post office for the Armies in the West and they will come quicker by being sent to that point.

After about one month of picket duty in and around Jackson, Tennessee, the 114th was sent back to Memphis to guard the Memphis & Charleston Railroad. They had yet to engage in any battle. By returning to their camps in Memphis the men finally had their tents to sleep in. The tents were left behind when they set out for Mississippi in November and therefore the soldiers had slept in the open for two and half months of winter, except for the times they found shelter in barns or warehouses.

During his month in Memphis Newton found time to write several letters home. He reiterates his opposition to the Emancipation Proclamation and claims that his sentiments are shared by most of the Union soldiers. He inquires about friends and family back home in Beardstown, gives prices of "nicknacks" in Dixie, longs to eat "a fat coon or some coon oil bisquit", and talks about the naval warfare going on in the Mississippi River between Union and Confederate gunboats.

Memphis, Tennessee, February 2, 1863

Dear Brother [William]: It is with pleasure I take my pen to answer your kind letter of January the twenty third. I was very glad to hear that you were well but was sorry to hear that Sister Margaret was so unwell. I am well and I hope this will find you all the same. I was very glad to get your letter this evening for I expect that we will leave Memphis in the morning. We are ordered to march with thirty days rations. We are to go south by land and you may be asured that we will have some pretty marching to do, but thats what we went a souldiering for. Their has been a great many troops went down the river lately. I suppose they are going to pay Mobile a visit. You say that you have bought that land from Fish[37], and you want to know how or on what terms you are to till the land, and for my part all I have to say is go ahead and do the best you can. And what ever you think is rite I am willing, for you know in what order the land and fencing is in and all I want to is to know how you get along until I return to Illinois. I think you got the land on reasonable terms enough and it appears that you did not have to pay a great deal down to commence with. I havent any idea that I will visit Illinois this year unless the war would play out and and I havent mutch [hope] that it will but still it might and again it might not. My time will be half out the eleventh of this month. The weather here is very nice for the time a year. The boats are running very lively on the river. I havent any war news to write this time but I expect to have a plenty to write pretty soon if things goes on all rite down here in Dixie for the Spring campaign will soon commence in this section of the country. Joseph Barwick[38] is here to day. He is well and a fine looking souldier.

---

37 Probably Ebenezer Fish who owned a mill in Cass County, Illinois.

38 Joseph Barwick originally enlisted on August 21, 1861, and then reenlisted as a veteran in the Third Cavalry on March 15, 1864. He was mustered out as a corporal on October 10, 1865. (*Barwick)

The troops have all come in from Corinth. Lieut. Hawyer and Co. are here in town. I sent you twenty dollars the other day by George Rienbarger[39] but I expect he is up there by this time. You must excuse this mixed up letter for the boys are all in the barracks [and] keeps up a perfect muss all the time. I will bring this to a stop by saying write soon. Yours, A. N. Paschal

Camp near Memphis, February 15, 1863

Dear Sister[Mary]: It is with pleasure I take my pen this morning to answer your kind letter of the date of Jan the 30. I was glad to hear from you all and that you were all well. I am well at the present time and hope this will find you all the same. We left Jackson a week ago yesterday or rather today. We got on the cars early Saturday morning and started but when we got at the outer edge of town the engine was thrown off the track by a switch that must of been some what out of repair. The engine was completly smashed. The front car was thrown from the track, the second car knocked the hind end off of the front one, and on by the third stopped on the track opsit where the engine fell. The grade was about four feet high. It was lucky it wasnt any higher. Their was no lives lost or any one hurt. We got on another train Sunday morning and left the old reck and landed safe at Memphis that night. We expect to camp here until they settle things down at Vicksburg to hold this part of the country. They say that they have got all the troops down there they want. Part of the Third Cavalry is here at Memphis. I saw Farrel Wells[40] yesterday. He is just about as fat as a pig ever gets. Thomas Cuppy[41] is not with his Co.

---

39   George M. Rhineberger (82nd Illinois Regiment, Company A). (*Rhineberger)

40   William E. "Farrell" Wells (3rd Cavalry, Co. F). (*Wells)

41   Thomas M. Cuppy had lived with the Jarratt Bridges Paschal family since before he was 10 years old. Research has not revealed whether he was an orphan, but he was, in essence, raised by the Jarratt Paschal family. Thomas had enlisted in the

Wells said that they left him at some where at a town sick and he had forgoten where. The weather is tollerable cool yet we had a snow about a week ago about 6 inches deep but it did not last for it commensed raining pretty soon after the snow fell and has been raining pretty near all the time since. But the sun is shining to day. I am very sorry that you have had such a bad muddy winter up north and have not had the pleasure of sleigh riding but you must try to compose your selves the best you can and let sleighing go. I guess you have got a saddle and bridal. Just go and saddle up Old Black Hawk and get you a good switch and take a pleasure ride. I can amagin now just how you would look. Tell Tommy that I promised to get him a pair of scats[42] this winter but I had forgotten it until now and I fear the winter is to near gone now for them to do him much good but if scating is good yet, tell Tommy to tell Joe and he will get them for him. Tell Will to not work to hard if he can help it for I expect his work will all come at once in the spring on account of such bad roads through the winter season. Their was one man died in our Co a little over a week ago by the name of Jesse E. Dunaway.[43] That was the first death in our Company. The health of the Regt is generaly good. I will stop writing for the present. Write soon. So no more at present.

Yours with respect, A.N.Paschal

P.S. Tell Will that I will write to him in about a week. Direct to Cairo.

Third Cavalry, Co. C, on August 19, 1861. Thomas wrote three letters (reprinted for the first time in this edition) to Mary Elizabeth Paschal. The letters express his strong fondness for her and, since she continues to inquire about him, the feeling may have been mutual. Thomas' military records state only that, on January 28, 1863, he left on a hospital boat near Vicksburg, Mississippi, but do not reveal his ultimate fate. It is presumed he died. (*Cuppy)

42   skates

43   Jesse E. Dunaway (114th Ill, Co. A) was 42 years old when he enlisted as a corporal. He left at home his wife, Margaret, and five children, Ann, Parris, Thomas, William and Jennie. He died at Jackson, Tennessee, on February 6, 1863.

Camp Near Memphis, Tennessee, February 22, 1863

Dear Brother [William]: It is with pleasure I take my pen to write you a small letter to let you know that I am well and hope this will find you all the same. I received the Central Illinoian[44] yesterday that you sent me of the date of Jan the 29. It was a considerable time a coming but it found me at last. It must of went out to Jackson, the place that we were encamped at before we came here. I was glad to get a paper from Beardstown even if it is a pour thing. It is just about as good as could be expect of Lu Reavis. Their was some sketches in it that interested me very much especly Mr. Epler[45] in the legislature. I think that he has played hob with his ducks and ought to have his neck stretched for his conduct. Mr. Fish made some terable mistakes in his letter to the Illinoian. In the first place he headed it Jackson, Mississippi, when it should of been Tennessee. And speaking of a depredation being commited on a good Union made by breaking open his store is false, but their was a sesesh store broke into by a Minisota Reg and they made a pretty good haul. He said the store was broken open by a squad of the 22nd Illinois. Their was no such regiment at Paris[46] at all. He made several other blunders to numeras to mention. We havent been payed any yet and dont know when we will be. This Reg is a getting tired of this way of souldiering. Six months with out any pay and they swear they wont stay much longer in the army without they get their pay. They are a getting tired of the way things are going on any way. All of the troops are opposed to freeing the slaves. The souldiers has come to the conclusion that they

---

44 The Central Illinoian, originally called The Gazette was published in Beardstown, Illinois at the time of the Civil War by L. U. Reaves. John S. Nicholson became the editor in 1867.

45 James Milton Epler (born 22 April 1833) was a Representative to the Illinois Legislature from 1862 to 1868. He held the office of State Senator from 1868 to 1872. On 29 March 1855, he married Nancy A. Epler.

46 Paris is located in Henry County, Tennessee, about 60 miles northeast of Jackson.

*are a fighting for the slave instead of the union and it would
be hard to make them believe any thing else. Unless the troops
are properly informed what the goverment intends to do, if
they entend to free the slaves, they had better tell the troops
what they intend to do with them, wether they intend to let
them go north or not, and unless this is done pretty soon you
need not look for any thing encouraging from our army. The
men dont actually know what they are a fighting for. So you
can judge from this what kind of a fix our troops are in. Their
has been victories lost already on this account. If they intend
to carry this war out for the purpose of freeing the slaves they
had better let it be known and let the men know what they
are a doing. This thing of making souldiers think they are a
fighting for one thing and actualy fighting for another wont
win it, and the nature of men to be fooled with in this way,
when they are sensable of their misery or at least think they
are. I was in hopes that I would that never have to write such
a letter as this but the way things are I am compelled to do
so to tell the truth. Further more it is very nice to talk about
up north that taking the slaves away from the south would be
the quickest way to bring her back in to the union but such
doctrene as that wont do. It wont fill the bill. They cannot ever
bring the south in to the union in that way. Their might be
some hope of bringing the south back in to the union if they
would let slavery alone but as long as they keep up the niger
question their will never be peace in the United States and
it will entirely distroy our goverment if it is kept up mutch
longer. I dont think the south is as near whiped as she was
twelve months ago. She shows no signes of comeing back in
to the union at all. The citizens around here say the indipen-
dence of the south is clost at hand. They think about the first
of May will tell the tale but I think if things could be worked
rite they would turn their tune so it would sound a little
different from that in a little time. I think that if Vicksburg
falls in to our hands it will make the seseshers whistle through*

their teeth. So no more on the war at present. I wrote a letter to Mary a few days ago, also one to Joe. I would like to see you all very well but that is imposable at the present. I get along souldiering mutch better than I ever expected I could before I joined the army. I would get along firstrate if I could get out of the notion of hunting ducks, ketching fur and sutch amusements as that, and another thing I am getting tired of our grub. It is not sutch as I want altogather by any means. I like to have a change once and a while but it is one thing all the time. I would like to have a fat coon or some coon oil bisquit or something of that sort. I missed apples this winter and ther rarities. I will tell you what nicknacks is worth down here. Apples 5cts apease, pigs feet 15cts each, butter 50cts lb, eggs 50cts doz, whiskey 50cts pt, tobacco 2.50 lb, and Cheese 50 lb, and other things acording. Only souldeiring that keeps at the same old price, thirteen dollars a month, and shanty board and cooks it yourself, payable at the pleasure of the goverment. I believe that I will stop writing for this time. Yours with respect, A. N. Paschal PS. Please answer soon. I send my love to the whole family. I would like to have another Illinoian or too. I expect that we will stay here for some time. If nothing hapens we are expecting an attack at this place when the roads gets good so as the sesesh can travel, but let em cum, we are prepared for them. This sheet is full.

Camp Near Memphis, Tennesee March 3, 1863

Dear Brother [William]: I pick up my pen to write you a few words to let you know that I am well and to answer yours of Febuary the 22. I was glad to hear from you and that you were all well. I wrote you a letter a few days ago but I thought it wouldnt be amiss to answer the last letter I recieved. You spoke of a wedding or two that had come of in that neighbor hood and then you said their was a good prospect of [one] closser home. You thought that you had that secret to your self but you will find out that it leaked out. I saw Farrel Wells yesterday and he told me that their was a prospect of his being a little connected to me and before I took the hint you gave in your letter I asked him in what respect. Why he said my sister Liz[47] and your brother Bill is about to get married. So you see by this that I wasent as much in the dark on that subject as you suposed. I reckon that Old Jacob and Drusy[48] will have a nice dinner prepared. Oh how I regret that I am not there to shiveree you but I think that Tommy will shoulder up my old shot gun and go up and give you a round. I would never a thought that you and her would of made a match but since it is so I shall be mannered and wish you much joy. It looks like their is nothing now a days imposable. I expect the first thing I know one of those days I will hear of Mother and Old Beals[49] a getting married. But your marrying Liz Wells is some pumkins. I hope you dont allow to leve home and leve Mother, Mary and Blake[50] on the farm by themselves. I think that you had better stay on the farm even if you do marry, but you are your own man and I expect that you will have to do as you please. I would give you a little advise but I expect you think that you know about as much as I do so I will not send it in this letter. I will wait until I get the particulars of your wedding. I havent any thing to write that is encouraging conserning the war, rather to the reverse. The rebels has

---

47 Farrell Wells' sister, Elizabeth. There is no record that this marriage occurred. (*Wells)

48 Jacob and Drusilla Wells, the parents of Farrell Wells and Elizabeth Wells. (*Wells)

49 The Alvord Beals family was a close neighbor of the Paschal family. Like Newton's mother Sarah Paschal, whose husband Coleman died in August of 1852, Mr. Beals' wife Charlotte had died on March 29, 1853. Mr. Beals had been born in Plainfield, Massachusetts on July 8, 1795. Perhaps the children teased their mother about marrying Mr. Beals. Mr. Beals died in 1870 and is buried beside his wife in Thomas Beard Cemetery in Cass County, Illinois.

50 "Blake" was Newton's nickname for his youngest brother, Tommy.

captured the Queen of the West[51] and the Indianola[52] and have them at work, against us. We are expecting every day to hear of their making an attack on our transport vessels and if they would I dont see any thing to hinder them from having their own fun. We are of the opinion almost to a man that the Union is gone up without a doubt. Their has been to much parshality used amoung our officers for things to prosper and their has been to much partiality shown towards the Negro. I dont think that God ever entended that the Negroes should be free and on the same footing with the white men as the greater part of the Abolitionists wants them, and if they ever do free them they will have to do it themselves. They cant do it with the army that is now in the field thats certain. They are to badly mixt up. If the men that is in the field was all abolitionests it would do for the President to present emancipation proclomations but it wont do with the army that is now in the field. I consider if the south gaines her independence it is the fault of the men that is at the head of our goverment for meadling with slavery when our goverment or rather our Union was in so mutch danger. I have heard it exprest several times since I enlisted, by a certain party, [that] we will free the slaves or ruin our country. Now such sentiments as them wont take out of that party and the men that utters them even if it is their sentiments. They are fools to let it be openly known unless they were certain that they could acomplish and bring about the desired efect. This war kinder gets me and I think it would get a wooden man. This is my idea about it. This army of ours will have to be divided into two parts - them that wants to fight for the slaves will have to go to them selves and fight for the slaves, and them

---

51 On February 14, 1863, while engaging Confederate batteries, the Queen of the West went aground. With the steampipe severed the vessel had to be abandoned. The commander, Charles Ellet, blamed the loss of the Queen on a disloyal pilot.

52 On February 24, 1863, on the Mississippi, the Federal gunboat Indianola was attacked by four Confederate vessels, including the previously-captured Queen of the West. After numerous rammings, Lieut. Comm. George Brown, surrendered the partially sunken vessel.

*that wants to fight for the Union and not for the freedom of
the slaves will have to go to themselves. And by making this
division it will make three armies of a vast difference of opinion
for then the weakest party would be apt to get whiped pretty
soon and then their might be some chance of peace. Where
their is a fuss between only two persons their is some hopes of
them a getting on good terms again but when the third one
puts his nose in, it allways makes the fuss ten times worse. I
would explain this further but it is getting dark so I will wind
up for this time. Write soon. Yours with respect A N Paschal*

Camp near Memphis, Tennessee, March 10, 1863

*Dear Sister [Mary]: It is with pleasure I take my pen in hand
this morning to write you a few lines to let you know that I am
well at present and hope this will find you all the same. We are
still at our camp but we are under marching orders to be ready
to march at an hours notice, but when that notice will come is
more than I can tell. The order may be countermanded and we
may not move at all. Such things is often the case. The weather
is very disagreable down hear. It is cold and rainy. It is raining
today just about rite. It makes the boys stay in the tents pretty
close. Wm Crow is still in Memphis. I havent heard from him
for three or four days. If he dont come out in two or three
days I will go and see him. I heard yesterday that Mr. Joseph
Lightfoot and Miss Mat Treadway[53] was going to get married
in a short time. I want you to tell them both that I wish them
mutch joy, happiness and prosperity. Our Regiment got a little
pay yesterday. They got pay for two and some days. I paid
my sutler bill[54] which was the enormas sum of one dollar and
had thirty three dollars and 20 cts left. Some of the boys owed*

---

53 Joseph C. Lightfoot married Martha A. Treadway on March 12, 1863, in Cass
County, Illinois. (*Lightfoot)

54 Sutler is a term used to refer to the "company store" or provisioner.

the sutler as high as sixten dollars. Their was a fellow started from here this morning for Cass County by the name of A. J. Saylor[55]. *He lives four miles below Skinners and I sent Hazen Skinner*[56] *a letter by him and in Skinner's letter I sent you one and told him the first time he went to Beardstown to take it to Ira Crow*[57] *and leave it there for you. In that letter I put twenty eight dollars in green backs. If Saylor gets off from Memphis today he will get home in about a week. I would have sent my money by Boemler*[58] *but he was not a going to start back in less than a week and besides he will have enough of things to take any way. And if anyone sends any thing by express he has to close it if any thing hapens to it, so I thought that I would send it the easiest way. To send money through the post offices is uncertain business and if that dont go safe it will learn me not to send any with him any more thats all. It is a small amount any way and if you get it I would like for you to put it on interest. It is handy with out to much danger of loosing it. We will be apt to get pay again in about a month or two at the farthest if we dont get where the sesesh are so thick that the pay masters will be a feard to venture in. I am very thankful that my health has been pretty good ever since I enlisted. Seven months is almost gone and I havent had to go in to battle yet. We have been pretty lucky in that respect but we have earnt our money a marching and exposure thats sertain. Vicsburg is not taken yet. So no more at present. Write as soon as you get this or that other letter before mentioned, so I will wind this up. Yours truly A. N. Paschal*

---

55 Abraham J. Saylor (82nd Illinois, Co A) (*Saylor)

56 Hazen Skinner was the husband of Newton's deceased sister, Harriett.

57 Newton's uncle, Ira Crow, was married to Rebecca Street, his mother's youngest sister.

58 Lewis Boemler (114th Ill, Co A), may have been a courier. He was mustered out on August 3, 1865. (*Boemler)

On March 4, 1863, Captain John Johnson of Company A took 25 of his men, possibly including Newton, south of the Memphis encampment with orders to destroy a bridge on Nonconnah Creek and further obstruct the road so that Confederates could not transport artillery toward the city. According to W.A. Mallory the men of Company A "destroyed the bridge, barricaded the road with trees and returned to camp without any casualty."

Their flank thus protected the men of the 114th Illinois left Memphis on Tuesday, March 17th aboard transport boats down the Mississippi River. They were headed for Young's Point, Louisiana to join the First Brigade, First Division, Fifteenth Army Corps, under the command of Major General William Tecumseh Sherman. Sherman had 32,000 men under his command as he approached Vicksburg via the Mississippi River and adjoining water routes. Meanwhile, Major General Ulysses Grant, with 40,000 troops, approached by land in a roundabout way to keep the Confederates uncertain of his plans.

Newton wrote home to his brother the following night as the regiment camped on a small island a few miles south of Helena, Arkansas. Newton refers to the encampment as "The Devil's Half Acre". W.A. Mallory described it as "A strip of land covered with a young growth of cottonwood. We were crowded so closely that the tents were touching all over the island, with only a few narrow tortuous ways for streets."

Camp 6 miles below Helena, Arkansas, March 18, 1863

Old Grub [William]: I am a going to write you a few lines to let you know that I am well at present and hope this will find you all the same. We are a waiting here for small boats to go down through the Yazoo Pass but the General thinks it will be about two weeks befour this division will get off from this place. Their is about 80 thousand men in this Camp. Will Crow is still at Memphis. I saw him a few days ago. He is getting better. He would of come to the Reg if we had not been comeing down the river. Most of the boys dont like the idea of going down to Vicksburg. I saw one of my cousins yesterday.

One of Wash Thomases[59] boys. He is in the 93 Reg Illinois, Co F. He looked stout and hearty. I wrote Mary a letter about a week ago and I sent 28 dollars about the same time by a young man by the name of A. J. Saylor and told him to give it to Hazen Skinner. He lived between Skinners and Meridosh[60]. It is getting tolerable warm down here these days and I dont like it any of the best. I havent heard of any fighting lately but I expect to befour long. Their has been three deserted out of our Company, Thos Williams[61], Louis Meyer[62] and George White[63], and two out of Co. D, Frank Looker[64] and Van Harris[65]. I havent had a letter from any of you since the first of March and that letter was the one with 25 cents in it. I have written several lately. The mail will be very unregular down here I expect and uncertain but if we get into a fight and get out again I will try and let you know how Joe made it. But I hope Vicksburg will get taken before we get down there. I wouldnt mind going down there if it wasnt so hot and sticky. The water is very high down here. If it raises much more it will dround out the southern Confederacy and it may dround befour I will help it out thats certain. I dont know whether it will be of any use for me to direct my letters to Beardstown to you much longer for expect that you will get drafted before long and

---

59   George Washington Thomas was married to Mary Paschal. Their son, Francis Marion Thomas (93rd Illinois, Co. F) enlisted on July 30, 1862, from Whiteside County, Illinois, and was mustered out June 23, 1865, with the rank of corporal. (*Thomas)

60   Meredosia is a small town in Morgan County, Illinois, on the Illinois River.

61   Thomas H. Williams (114th Ill, Co. A) enlisted September 1, 1862, and deserted March 11 1863. (*Williams)

62   Louis Meyer (114th Ill, Co. A) enlisted August 14, 1862 and deserted March 11, 1863. (*Meyer)

63   George Washington White was mustered out on August 3, 1865. There is no evidence in the Adjutant General's Report that George White deserted.

64   Franklin Looker (114th Ill, Co. D) was from Virginia, Cass County, Illinois. He enlisted on August 15, 1862, and deserted March 11, 1863.

65   Martin Van Buren Harris (114th Ill, Co. D) was mustered in as a corporal on August 26, 1862. He mustered out on August 3, 1865, as a private. (*Harris)

course south, but I hope that Illinois wont stand a draft unless it is got up a little different to the present one but if you do get it poked to you I want you to let me know. So no more at present. Yours truly, A N Paschal Write soon.

The Devil's Half Acre, March 23, 1863, Four Miles Below Helena, Arkansas

Dear Brother: It is with pleasure I take pen in hand to answer your kind letter of March the eight. was glad to hear from you and that you were all well. I am well and hope this will find you all the same. I havent anything of any importance to write at present. The weather has been very nice for the last two weeks but it changed last night and is raining this morning about rite. The river is still rising and if it raises as much in the next five days as it has the last five it will make us leve this Camp thats certain. We havent had any news from Vicksburg lately. We are in sight of the Yazoo Pass but its on the write side of the river from us. I think that we will have the pleasure of taking a trip down it pretty soon, but a souldier never knows where he is going until he gets there and hardly then. Their is one thing sertain we cant do any marching down here on foot until the water falls. We are a having an easy time at this camp. It is surrounded by water and we dont have any guard and their aint any room to drill. That suits me you bet. The timber is nice and green, peach trees are in full bloom and have been for two weeks. I get in a canoe and cruise round pretty near every day and that is grand sport for me. Their has been more work done on canoe digging than I ever heard tell of in so short time. If you will come down here after we leve, you can get the best lot of hog traughes you ever heard tell of. Lots of the boys that dont know much about small boats gets plenty of ducking in the water. The boys makes a practice of dunking every officer that they can get out in a canoe and thats lots of fun. I saw Cousin Marion Thomas yesterday. His brigade left here last night and I dont know whether it went in the Pass or not. He is in the 93rd Co F Ills Vol 7 Division and we are in the 8 Division. His regiment [was] to be in our brigade but it got out some way or other. We have no idea of the war closing any ways soon, if ever. The boys are a making great calculations what they will do when their three years expires but I think that is foolishness to think of what they will do that far ahead. And their is another thing I cant help but notice. The men that was the most religeous at home are the worst men we have in camp and the men that was the worst at home are the civilest in camp. Boys that ust to swear very hard at home have pretty near quit it entirely. A sutler makes money the easiest of any one in the army and the most of it they generaly sell about one hundred dollars worth of stuff for one thousand. Their is generaly as large a crowd around a sutler shop as their is around a ticket wagon at a big show. Lots of the boys dont send any money home at all and they spend it all with the sutlers. I sent twenty eight dollars home if it ever gets there and if it does not it wont be mutch loss to me while I am in the survice of Uncle Sam, but if I should be so lucky as to live through this war and get back home safe it wouldent be bad. [You] seemed to think a load of mellons would pay down here and I am of the same opinion. Just bring down a load and I will bye one at most any price if you will take Green Backs but if you calculate on getting silver or gold for them you had better not start. I think that Mary has forgotten all about me or else she would write a little oftner but I expect she doesent have much time to write to any one for I expect that she has considerable work to do, especially a doing up shirts for you. I am glad that Blake went to school so regular last winter if he did not go against his will. I expect Blake will be sidling up to the girls pretty soon and writing love letters, but like you I am a getting to be quite an Old Batch myself. I havent shaved since I left home, only with the sisors. I am sunburnt about as yellow as a punken and look more like Old Phelps than any one else I can think of that you are acquainted with. I wouldent mind souldiering mutch if they would let me do as I pleased and go where I pleased but this thing of serving a boss is what gets the worst and the thoughts of doing two years and a half yet sums it all up together [and] it makes quite a dose to swallow. Sutch times as those being swore in and mustered in to survice was considered a small dose last August but here is March and some of the Boys are a getting pretty sick of that dose you bet. A great many bit at the bait because it had a tail to it and that tail was unless sooner discharged. But it appears in biting at the tail they got hooked in with that animal that is called three years. It appears as if they quit biting at bait up north entirely so Old Abe has got a kinder of sain[66] now pretty near ready for use. I see he alows to ketch fish whether they will bite or not and succers apears to be a favorite fish with him or at least he uses quite a number of them and still wants mor. He has allready got over his quota in that state and I think there would be pollicy for him to draw his sain in some other puddle at present unless he wants to catch some of the old copperheaded tough cuses that ant worth any thing any where, but maybe he can put them to some use. I have got this letter tangled up and I will stop. Write soon. So no more at present. Yours truly, A. N. Paschal. To Wm H. Paschal.

From the overcrowded island the men moved on down the Mississippi towards Young's Point. Most of Sherman's forces were encamped at Young's Point, Lake Providence, or Milliken's Bend. The 114th was en-camped at Duckport, about six miles north of Young's Point. Duckport was a deserted plantation. According to Mallory the officers took over two plantation homes and "a village of neat negro houses." From Duck-port the men of the 114th would help dig a canal for Union gunboats to enter the Mississippi below Vicksburg without running the gauntlet of Confederate boats protecting the river.

---

66   seine, a large fishing net.

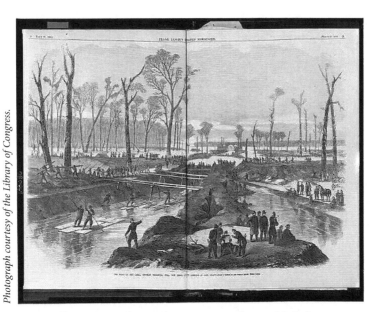

Illustration of men digging a canal near Vicksburg.

This strategy, which Grant conceded was mainly employed to keep his men busy, did not work. Union boats, under the command of Rear Admiral David Glasgow Farragut, also attempted to approach Vicksburg, "The Gibraltar of the Confederacy", from the north via the Yazoo River. When this route proved impregnable the XV Corps began digging more futile canals to various bayous and also planned a canal from Lake Providence to the Red River. The men of the 114th assisted in digging a canal in the Bayou Macon that was eventually three miles long and 40 feet wide. Mallory reported to the Illinois Journal that, "About a dozen barges and a very small steamboat passed through the canal." But, he continued, "The river is falling so rapidly that the canal will be dry in another week."

Duckport, Louisiana, April 4, 1863

Dear Sister [Mary]: It is with pleasure I take my pen to answer your kind letter of March the 14 which gave me great pleasure to hear from you. I am not very well but am getting better. I

*have got the quick step. I supose it was caused by drinking to
much river. The boys as a general thing are in good health.
We are within 7 mile of Vicksburg by land & twelve by water.
I have no news of mutch importance to write. The weather is
very nice. It is just about as warm as it is in Illinois in May or
the 1st of June. This is a low flat country down hear. I expect if
we stay down here any length of time we will be apt to get the
ague and I expect that mosquitoes will by pretty thick down
here shortly. I cant see any signs of an attack being made on
Vicksburg any ways soon. Their was a fleet went up the river
day before yesterday of 20 boats loaded with souldiers but I
have not found out yet where they were going. We are on the
west side of the river in the State of Louisiana. We came down
the Mississippi River. The Yazo Pass has turned out a failure.
They are a cutting a new canal on this side of the river to get
below Vicksburg.[67] It will be completed on a few days. I do not
think it is the intention of our Generals to attack Vicksburg
at all if they can take it any other way. They are a trying to
get their troops all round the place and cut off their supplies
and cause them to come out or starve. Wm Crow is still at
Memphis. I heard from him yesterday. He has got the measles
and is in the hospital in the convilesent fort. You spoke in your
letter of Mr Richard[68]. I saw him at Memphis. He looked stout
and hearty and said he liked souldiering fine, but he is like
every body else. He would like to see it stop. I am in hopes that
we wont have to stay down in this hot climate all summer.*

---

67 Major General John Alexander McClernand had been ordered to march south on
the west side of the Mississippi to New Carthage, Louisiana, below Vicksburg. A
final canal was being built, known as the Duckport Canal.

68 William Richard (3rd Ill Cavalry, Co. F) of Beardstown, Illinois was born in 1827 in
Pennsylvania. He enlisted on August 19, 1861, with the rank of corporal and mustered out on September 15, 1864, as Company Quartermaster Sergeant. Mary frequently inquires as to "Mr." Richard's whereabouts and exhibits a genuine concern
for his welfare. We do not know the reasons for her frequent inquiries or why she
(and Newton) refers to him as "Mr." Richard. Since he was older, he may have been
someone of authority or responsibility in their lives prior to the war. Mr. Richard
died in 1904 and is buried in the Grove Hill Cemetery in Morrison, Illinois. Two
brothers of Coleman Paschal, William and John, are also buried in Morrison.

I expect if it gets too hot down here for me I will let my legs help me out of the sunny south for I dont intend to be eat up with the mosquitoes if I can help it, but I intend to stay in the army as long as I can stand it without suffering to much or exposing health to any great extent. Their aint any show for a single man to get a furlow unless he can prove that he is a true abolitionist and will support the party in every respect. The abolitionests in our regiment has got so smart that they got to calling all of the democrats copperheads and it has caused several black eyes amongst the boys and if it is kept up it will cause several more. It is the prettiest sight I ever saw to look out on the river at the boats those nice mornings. Sometimes their are a hundred in sight. The most of our wounded are being sent up the river to Memphis and other points. I wish that I could give you the particulars of the fight but I cant tonight. It is nip and tuck like a dog in wool but I think our men are a getting the best of the bargain. Our shells are doing considerable damage to their city and if it is kept up mutch longer they will burn it up. I will answer Joe's letter in a day or two if I stay at camp. I expect that you have a fine time a running around with the fair sex but that is your privilege not mine. At present girls are scarce here in the country but their are plenty in Vicksburg and I calculate to see them before long if we dont get a backset of some kind. The prisnors say their are some mighty good looking ones and lots of them, and we can make Union women out of some of them. Some of them are already since their men folks was conscripts and they had to go there to live. I hope this war will close this summer but I hardly think it will. I have had a fine time for the last month. I ketch plenty of fish, get plenty of honey, buy pies at ten cents a peace & lager beer at 10 cts a glass. But I cant get any whiskey at all. Tobacco is very high but I still use the weed. It is geting late so I will stop scratching. Write soon.

Yours With Respect, A. N. Paschal

April 5, 1863

Weather very nice. Our Reg is at work on the canal today. I am cook for our mess today and get to stay in camp. We are encamped within three hundred yards of the canal. I saw a letter from Brooks to T . Brown the other day. It was a large letter but contained but little news except he gave a full history of Joe 's wedding[69] and said the rest of the family was well. H. Freeman[70] and U. Pedigo[71] are well. Lieut. Lucas[72] has not got back to the Company yet. A little German by the name of Haid[73] is acting in his place and makes a very good officer. I expect that we will be payed off again soon but if we are I dont know how we can send our money home. If I dont get a good way to send mine I will keep it until I do. I havent heard yet whether you got that I sent from Memphis. Their has always been a great talk about our men a having the Negroes at work a digging the canals down here but when we got down here we found out that was a mistake. Their are but very few negroes at work at all and what is are hired by the day or month and can quit when they please. Our army would be better off if they would drive every negroe out of it. But I dont see how the officers could get along with out them. Pretty near every Captain has one, Majors two, Colonels six, Brigadier Generals twelve, Major Generals twenty and the higher the office the more nigers they have to wait on them and all of these darkys has a easier time than the souldiers

---

69   The wedding of Joseph Lightfoot and Martha Treadway on March 12, 1863.

70   Henry D. Freeman was Newton's cousin. Lieutenant Henry D. Freeman of the 114th Infantry, Company D, Illinois Volunteers, was captured at the Battle of Brice's Cross Roads near Guntown, Mississippi, but escaped. See, letter by Henry Freeman printed later herein. (*Freeman)

71   Urban Pedigo (114th Ill, Co. D) married to Newton's cousin, Mary Catherine Paschal. (*Pedigo)

72   Philander Lucas (1st Lieut, 114th Ill, Co. A), from Beardstow n, Illinois. Resigned on October 15, 1964.

73   Frederick Haid (lst Sergeant, 114th Ill., Co. A) from Beardstown, Illinois. Musered out May 31, 1865.

and get as much pay and as much clothing and better things to eat. The officers think more of a darkey than they do of a private in the ranks a fighting for his country and this is more than I can put up with much longer thats so. You may think that I have turned out to be a Democrat or a Copperhead[74] or a sesesh but I am far from it as ever I was. I am still willing to fight for the Union but they cant stuff the doctrine down me that a negro is as good as a white man and I will as soon let this union go to ruin before I will consider the blacks my equal. If they intend to carry on this war and still intend freedom to negroes they will shortly have to carry it on without asistance from me for I will die rather than be put on an equal footing with the blacks. Write as soon as you get this. Yours with respect A. N. Paschal

April 5, 1863

Dear Brother [Tommy]: It is with pleasure that I take my pen to answer your kind letter I was very glad to hear from you and am very glad that you have been going to school. You are improving your education very fast. I was very sory to hear that Joe had been sick but was glad to hear he was better. I am glad you shivereed them new married folks. I want you and Grub to pitch in and make all you can this summer on the farm but dont work too hard. I want you to go to school all you can for a good education is worth a fortune to any man. I would like to see you all very well, but I have got a boss that wont let me run around to see my relatives mutch. But the time is passing off very fast. It is near eight months since I enlisted. I think that we will have some conscripts pretty soon to help us free nigers or fight for Uncle Sam just which ever you pleas to call it. I hope this war will close before hot

---

74   "Copperhead" was a Northerner sympathetic to the Confederacy.

weather but their are but little signs of it at the presant time. Their will be plenty of peaches and apples down here this season. Peaches are larger than haselnuts now. This is a great country for blackberies but their aint any strawberies. I saw Joe Sheler[75] today. He used to work for Ira Crow. Blake, I will quit for this time. Answer soon. So no more at present. Yours with respect, A. N. Paschal PS Tell Grub to write

Youngs Point, April 12, 1863

Dear Brother Grub [William]: It is with pleasure I take my pen to answer your kind letter of March the 29. I was glad to hear that you were all well. I am well and hope this will find you all the same. I have nothing of any importance to write at present I got a letter yesterday from Uncle Richard Wright[76]. They were all well. Our army is in good health as a genereal thing down here. The weather is very warm. It rained a very nice shower last night. The troops are a lying still and not doing much of anything. Their was three gun boats past down by here this morning. I think they will pitch in to Vicksburg pretty soon from all appearences. We have been at work on a canal about two weeks. It is about finished I think. It is the intention to send our division into Texas pretty soon to keep the Sesesh from gettting supplies from that place. If the Canal proves good it will enable us to get down to the mouth of Red River without passing by Vicksburg. I heard yesterday but havent heard what it was for. I saw David Shootman[77] this morning and Dan Cuppy[78]. Both of them belongs to the 11th Mo Reg. I havent heard from Cousin Marion Thomas since we

---

75 Joseph Sheeler married Sarah C. Fish on December 24, 1868.

76 Richard Wright was married to Newton's aunt, Joan R. Paschal, sister of his father.

77 David Shootman (Company I, 11th Regiment, Missouri Volunteers) was mustered out as a Lieutenant. (*Shootman)

78 Daniel Cuppy (Co. C, 11th Regiment, Missouri Volunteers). (*Cuppy)

left Helena. The division he belonged to went down the Yazoo
Pass but I heard since that they had backed out and was above
here on the Mississippi River. We have drew four mouths
more pay lately. Several of the boys sent their money home by
express but I did not send any. I did not want to run the risk at
the present time. I am a going to send two dollars in this letter
and send more the first good oppertunity. I think the Chaplain
or some one else will get a furlow pretty soon to go home and I
will get to send by them. I am out of postage stamps and they
are pretty hard to get down here. I wish you would send me a
few the next time you write. I can send a letter without them
but I dont think they are as apt to get through. You spoke of
Sam running off with you. He must be a getting pretty stout.
I think you had better hitch him up to a plow and put him
through awhile. I think that would cool him down a little. I
wrote Mary a letter a few days ago. I went a fishing this after
noon and caught a couple of mud cats about a foot long. I saw
an alagator that a fellow had killed. Their are plenty of them
fellows down here in the swamps. It is getting almost supper
time so I will dry up this letter. Write soon and give me the
news. So no more at present. Yours truly, A. N. Paschal

Duckport, Louisana, April 14, 1863

*Dear Sister [Mary]: It is with pleasure I resume my seat this
evening to answer your kind letter of March the 25th. I was
very glad to hear from you and the rest of the family. I have
nothing of any importance to write at present. I received your
letter about an hour ago, also one from Hazen Skinner. I
shouldnt of written this evening only orders came that their
wouldnt be any mail go north after today for some time. I
expect their will not be any more mail go north until after the
move on Vicksburg which I think will take place in a very few
days. Their is a report here today that Charleston is taken but*

not confirmed. I hope it is true but I have but little faith in rumors or newspapers now a days. The boys hates the idea of marching on to Vicksburg but they are willing to do any thing to end the war. Let it be hard or easy their is but little differ-ence. They do not stop the mail from coming South so you may answer as soon as you get this. I am well at presant and hope this will find you all the same. Their are but very few sick in Camp. We had a very heavy rain last night and their are good prospects for an other to night. The River is pretty high and raising slowly. The weather a little cooler and the mud about thick enough to make pan cakes out of and well mixed. I have got plenty of pocket change. We got four months pay. I sent Will a letter the other day and put two dollars in it and I will send two in this if ever gets there safe and if it does not it wont be much loss. I buy several nicknacks to eat since warm weather has set in for I think that they are healthier then so much strong diet but they come very high. I get them on the boats that come down the river. I buy butter, eggs, potatoes, onions, and dried fruit and the like and the most of the other boys does the same. We draw plenty of flower, pilot bread[79], sugar, coffee, tea, beans, bacon and some fresh beef & vinegar. I dont know whether our Division will be ordered to Vicksburg or out in Texas. I rather suppose the latter but if we go out their we will have a great deal of marching to do but I had just about as soon march as face the music at Vicksburg thats so. I hear a few bull dogs bark pretty near every day at a distance but I dont mutch fancy getting too clost. I am a feard it might sound more harsh in my ears. But let come what will. I am like one of the Dutch men in our Co said he was. I am swore in and have to go. This was written in haste it being the fifth letter I have written to day so I will quit this time with one small sheet poorly filled and I dont know how many mistakes. I will have to get it in the letter bag pretty soon, so no more at

---

79   Pilot bread or biscuit is another name for hardtack.

*present. Yours Truly, A. N. Paschal PS. Write soon and give
me the news. Tell the girls to write to me if they want to get
married for I never have ritten to a girl a letter yet but whilst
she got married in a short time afterwards.*

From April 29th through May 1st the XV Corps engaged in a diver-
sionary demonstration near Snyder's Bluff. The demonstration itself
was a bluff meant to draw Confederate attention away from Grant's
forces, approaching Jackson, Mississippi from the southwest. Jackson was a major supply station for Vicksburg. On May 2nd the 114th
began a 63-mile march over rough roads to reach Jackson and assist
Grant. Newton did not participate in this first action of the 114th. He
was "ailing" and left behind at Duckport "to cook for the boys that
wasn't able to cook."

The battle for Jackson was actually a series of small skirmishes since
the main body of Confederate troops had already abandoned the city.
A few rebel diehards kept up some artillery fire and the 114th reported
seven casualties. Jackson fell to Union forces on May 14th. Two days
later the 114th was engaged in the Battle of Champion's Hill on the
Big Black River east of Vicksburg, where Gen. Grant crushed the rebel
forces under the command of Gen. John C. Pemberton. The noose had
tightened on Vicksburg.

Following the Battle of Champion Hill Grant ordered his three corps
commanders; Maj. Gen. John McClernand (XIII Corps); Maj. Gen.
William T. Sherman (XV Corps) and Maj. Gen. James B. McPherson
(XVII Corps) to attack a series of redoubts protecting Vicksburg from
the east. Pemberton's rebel forces were able to repel wave after wave of
Union assaults while waiting in vain for reinforcements from General
Joseph Johnston. Johnston never made a serious move. He had given up
on Vicksburg.

Newton and the other men of the 114th left behind at Duckport could
not immediately rejoin their companies because of transportation prob-
lems. Newton expected to be sent to Young's Point to guard Confederate prisoners-of-war but on the very day he was scheduled for guard
duty he was sent down to Vicksburg to "carry dispatches to the north
boats acrost the bend of the river." He seems to have enjoyed his new

assignment because it allowed him to move around and he felt, "About as indipendent as a hog on ice."

On May 22nd the 114th fought rebels again near the Big Black River. Three of their men were killed and sixteen wounded. On May 25th Grant agreed to a two and a half hour cease-fire so that bloated and reeking corpses, some of them rotting on the hot battlefields for five or six days, could be buried. For the next month and a half Union forces would continue to bombard Vicksburg and wait for its defenders to give up. The citizens of Vicksburg were forced to seek shelter underground. Black men hired themselves out as cave diggers. The caves saved some lives, but did not make life more tolerable for the starving, yet defiant citizens. They would endure until all hope was gone.

During the siege Union soldiers, like Newton, found free time to write home and explore their new surroundings. Newton writes about the siege, and about the flora, fauna and girls of the South in these next nine letters (and partial letters), dated between May 3rd and July 1st, 1863.

Duckport, Louisiana, May 3, 1863

Dear Brother: It is with pleausre I take my pen to let you know that your letter is at hand of April the 19. It found me in tollerable health. I have just finished reading it. I was glad to hear that you all well. This is the first letter I have received written in April. I had almost come to the conclusion that you had quit writing entirely. I was kinder under the weather last week but am all rite again. The weather is very hot down here at present. Our Reg started on a march of four days last Saturday. They left all at camp that wasent well and being as I was ailing they left me to tend to the camp and to cook for the boys that wasnt able to cook. Their was 9 of our Company left in Camp. But their are but one of them much sick. That is a John Truebswasser[80]. He has got a fever of some sort. I

---

80   John Truebswasser recovered from this illness, but later died at Mound City on June 26, 1864. (*Truebswasser)

am a going to take him to the hospital in the morning if he isnt better. About all of the sickness we have down here is the diarhea. It is caused by drinking bad water. I havent much news in regard to the army. Their hasnt been anything of much importance expired in the last month that I know of. I have heard considerable canon lately, but havent heard the result. The most of it was below Vicksburg. I suppose it was our gun boats a shelling the seshesh batteries down their. Vicksburg hasent been attacked yet. There is a general move going at present. Their will be a attack on some point this I think. Our division has gone below Vicksburg to Carthage[81]. Their was a gunboat went up the Yazoo and fired two hundred and 50 shots at the battery at Haines Bluff and then returned again. She got struck 50 times but received no serious damage. She went up to try their strength at that point. The water has fell six feet in the river and spoilt our canal, but the roads are in pretty good order for traveling and we can get along without it. I went out and gathered a lot of dew berries this morning you bet they were nice. Melons are ripe to. I am a having a fine time now. I stay under a large shade tree in the heat of the day. I am a learning how to souldier in the shade and I like it the best. I havent heard from Will Crow lately, not since Joe was down their[82]. He hasnt come down the river yet. The mosqui-toes are getting pretty thick down here these nights. They make me think of the stable loft but that . . .

(The remainder of this letter was missing from the collection.)

---

81   "On the 2nd of May, the regiment left for the rear of Vicksburg, and, on May 14, was engaged in the battle of Jackson, Miss.--loss, 5 men killed and wounded. Arrived in rear of Vicksburg, May 18, and participated in the siege--loss, 20 men killed and wounded." Adjutant General's Report.

82   Seems to indicate that Joseph Paschal had visited his brother-in-law Will Crow in Memphis.

Duckport, Louisiana May 22, 1863

Dear Brother: It is with pleasure I take my pen to write you
a few lines in answer of your letter and to let you know that
I am well and hope this will find you all the same. News is
plenty in Camp. Vicksburg was attacked by our forces last
Saturday. They have been fighting 7 days & nights and it is hot
and heavy. Reports are faverable on our side. We have taken
Haines Bluff[83] & Jackson[84] & Grand Gulf[85] and got Vicksburg
surrounded on all sides and closing in slowly. Our army has
been gaining ground on them every day. We have taken a
great many prisnors and a number of guns. Our troops burnt
Jackson and left it, for they had rather fight than guard seshesh
property. Our Reg has been in one fight. Got 6 killed and 20
wounded. But I got this from a stranger and cant vouch for
its truth but it looks reasonable for our division was the boys
that took Jackson. The canon action has veen very heavy this
evening but has almost ceased to night. I wrote Mary a letter a
few days ago stating how I am to be left at this place. Sent ten
dollars in it. I will send ten in this. I wish that I could send you
the particulars of the fight but I cant to night but I will send
you the particulars at as early date as posible. The news here
is that Gen. Hooker[86] was defeated with heavy loss and many
killed and wounded[87]. I expect that our loss will be heavy. It
is reported light yet but I think from the noise they keep up
that lead is flying at times. The canons fired so much to day

---

83 On the 16th of May began the Battle of Champion's Hill, and by the 18th, the Union Army moved across the Big Black River between Jackson and Vicksburg, took Hayne's Bluff, and began its siege of Vicksburg.

84 On May 14, in a driving rainstorm, the Union army neared Jackson, Mississippi. Confederate General Joseph Johnston, with diminished forces, knew it was futile to attempt to hold the city and evacuated the capital.

85 Grand Gulf, on the Mississippi, was evacuated by the Confederates on May 3.

86 Brig. Gen. Joseph Hooker (1814-1879), from Maine, was Commander of the Army of the Potomac at the time of this letter.

87 General Joseph Hooker's Army of the Potomac had taken a battering at Chancellorville, Virginia during the first week of May.

*for about two hours that I couldnt count the shots. The firing
was mostly from our gunboats. The health of the souldiers are
improving. Their was a man died belonging to our Company
on the 20th inst[88] by the name of Henry Weber[89], a German.
Urban Pedigo is very low but signs of better. E. D. Lindsley is
knocking around Camp. Wm Crow hasnt came down yet. I
fear he has had a serious time with the measels. The weather
is very hot with frequent showers. The river still falling. I have
had an easy time since the 14 of this month But I am a going
to go down to Youngs Point in the morning [and] guard some
of the sesesh prisnors that has been sent to that place. Their are
five thousand five hundred of them. They will be sent to Chigo,
Ills[90] in a few days. I expect to go to the Reg in about a week if
it dont return to this place. We was ordered to join the Reg this
week but we could not get transporation. It is getting late so I
will stop writing. I will write soon again, so no more to knight.
A.N. Paschal P.S. Write soon.*

Duckport, Louisiana, May 27, 1863

*Dear Brother: I sit down to answer your letter and to let
you know that I am well and so are the most of the boys in
Camp. Their has been some deaths in Camp lately. Urban
Pedigo is dead[91], also Sgt. Downing[92]. Them are all that you
were acquainted with. I havent started to the Reg yet. I have
been below here oposite Vicksburg for the last five days but
have returned to Camp again. I was carrying dispatches to*

---

88 inst - in or of the present month

89 Henry Webber (114th Ill., Co. A) enlisted on August 11, 1862, and died at Duck-port, Louisiana on May 22, 1863.

90 Camp Douglas was near Chicago, Illinois.

91 Urban Pedigo died at Duckport, Louisiana on May 23, 1863.

92 Lieut. David N. Downing, 114th Illinois, Co. D., died at Duckport on May 23, 1863. (*Downing)

the north boats accrost the bend of the river. I was in a pretty clost place but come out safe. Some shells burst pretty clost but I dont think that any peace came any closer than ten feet of me. The fight is still going on at Vicksburg but I havent heard from there to day. The battle is a hard one you bet. I heard from the Reg late this eve. They are pitching in to the Rebels like a buck into doe. They have lost but few men yet. Our Co has four wounded. I will give you the names of them. John Webb[93] rite arm shot off, T. Taylor[94] in calf of leg, Kenchler[95] thy, Cordell[96] knee. None killed. I received a letter from you since I commensd this and was glad to hear from you all. I also got one from Jonathan Peters and family[97] and one from Miss Peems. Their is but little signs of the Vicksburg fight ending soon I think it will last about a month. The canons are booming lively to night. I have got so ust to the noise that I dont notice it half of the time. I cut a bee tree this eveing and got a fine mess of young bees and found another tree. I dont know when I will go to the Reg or dont care. I am just about as indipendent as a hog on ice. I am a feard that you and Mary havent all of the letters that I sent. I have sent about thirty five dollars in letters since I have been down here. I would like for you to mention in your next how mutch of it has got through. I will not send any more until I hear from [you]. The most of it has had time to get there if it ever does. I am a getting to lazy to write but I will try to answer all letters I get. I dont expect that I will get to cum home this summer. Furlows has played out. The weather is very hot with thunder showers. The Rebels

---

93   John Webb (114th Ill, Co. A) was discharged on July 20, 1863, for disability. (*Webb)

94   T. Taylor is probably the Zachariah Taylor in Company A, 114th Illinois Regiment. He mustered out June 6, 1865. (*Taylor)

95   Edward E. Kenchler (114th Ill, Co. A), because of his wounds, was discharged on December 19, 1863. (*Kenchler)

96   Collen Cordell died at Memphis, Tennessee on June 7, 1863.

97   Newton's sister, Rachel, was married to Nathaniel Peters.

sunk our gun boat Cincinnatti[98] today. Before she went down she sunk in shallow watter and will be very easy raised. There was one killed on board & three wounded. Our men are all in good spirits. . . . [Remainder of letter lost]

Camp near Vicksburg, June 1, 1863

Dear Sister [Mary]: I again resume my pen to write you a few lines in answer to your kind letter of May the twenty ninth. I was very glad to hear from you all and hope this will find you all the same. I havent any thing of much importance to write at present for I havent red any news papers lately. The Rebels still hold Vicksburg but we hold the Country all around them. The Rebels are pretty spunky and hold out well. I wouldent wonder if we dident have some fun yet before we get Vicksburg. The Rebels are a consentrating a large forse about forty miles east of here with the intention of cutting their way through to Vicksburg but if they do undertake it their will be some pretty hard fighting but let them come, we are well prepared for them. We have been reinforsed by Burnside[99] with his whole army. I have no idea how many men we have at this place but I think we have a number sufficient to hold this place against any force that Old Jeff[100] can send in this direction. Vicksburg had a great deal better fortifications than was antisipated by our troops. They got sight of them [and could see] it would be almost impossible

---

98 An attempt was made to reduce Fort Hill, a Confederate stronghold on the Mississippi River, with the aid of gunboats. The Cincinnati, with added logs and bales of hay as protection, engaged the Confederate batteries; however, their higher position enabled them to shell the gunboat. She sank, her colors still flying, with forty casualties.

99 Maj. Gen. Ambrose Everett Burnsides (1824-1881), native of Indiana, was commanding the Department of the Ohio at the time of this letter. He had been Commander of the Army of the Potomac from November 1862 through January 1863.

100 Newton is, of course, irreverently referring to Jefferson Davis (1808-1889), Kentucky native, who was President of the Confederacy.

to take the place by storm. It may take several days yet. Our
men still keep up a pretty good noise a throwing shells into
the City. The weather still keeps very warm and disagreeable.
I wish this war would wind up so I could get out of this hot
climat but I dont want it to stop until the Union is restored.
I like this Country for its fruit, pretty trees and pretty flowers
and high hills. The Magnolia tree that grows here is the
prettiest tree in the world, also the Fig and the Cucumber
tree[101] and lotts of other things that is a show to me. I enjoy
my self mutch better than you might suppose I did but I
would be willing to leve the south with all of its curiosities if
the war was over and travel north. I was very sorry to hear
of the death of Aunt Emily Horn[102]. I would like to know how
Grand Pap[103] is getting along this summer. Henry Freeman
& James Berry[104] are both well. So no more at present.
Yours with respect, A. N. Paschal PS. Answer soon. Give my
respects to all inquiring friends. Good Bye for the present.

Camp near Vicksburg Miss, June 10, 1863

Dear Brother: I take my pen to answer your kind letter of May
the 24th. I was very glad to hear from you and that you were
all well. I am well at present and hope those few lines will find
you all the same. I am with the Reg. We are encamped eight
miles from Vicksburg on the Hains. We have been throwing
up brestworks to hinder reinforcements from coming in to
Vicksburg. We look to stand picket petty near all of the time.
We have a nice camp and plenty of plums and blackber-

---

101 A variety of American magnolia having fruit resembling a small cucumber.

102 Emily Paschal Horn, born 1807 in Wilson County, Tennessee, was a sister of New-ton's father, Coleman Paschal. She married Joel Horn on December 30, 1828.

103 Probably referring to his paternal grandfather, Isaiah Paschal, who was 82 years old at the time.

104 James Berry was married to Lucy A. Paschal, Newton's cousin. (*Berry)

ries but we have to carry water about a mile over the hills. We had a fine rain to day [and] the weather is very warm. Vicksburg is still in the hands of the Rebels but our troops are all around them and they cant get out. We have laid siege to the place and are feeding them on shot and shells. I think that we have got them foul but they are to big fools to think so or at least they dont let on. The Boys that was wounded in our Co are all doing well. I cant tell when Vicksburg will fall. I dont think it can hold out mutch longer. I think they will run short of provisins soon. I havent any news of any importance of any sort and am almost to lazy to write what little I do know. I told James Berry about his wife and boy[105]. James says he would like to be at home to see that little boy of his. I wrote a letter to Nathaniel Peters yesterday. I am getting used to the booming of canon. I dont fear them as mutch as I used to but they sound kinder harsh yet. They dont make nice music to dance after by considerable. I hope the war will dry up pretty soon, not because I dont like souldiering but I dont like to fool away so much time at one thing and I would like to get out of this hot climate. I am afraid that it is a going to be very sickly down here this summer. Our grub isnt any of the best. It is crackers and bacon, coffee, sugar & plums. But we get plenty of it so their is no danger of us starving. I was glad to hear that that five dollar bill got through safe. I have sent two ten dollar bills. I would like to hear of them getting home safe. They have had time to get there by this time. I am afeard to risk any more until I hear from that. I spend considerable money for nicknacks of one sort or other to eat this warm weather. I dont know when we will be paid again. I have got twenty dollars in my clothes and feel as independent as a hog on ice. It is rumored that their are thirty thousand Rebels coming in here in a day or two but they had better keep away if they know what is good for their health. I believe I have

---

105 James Berry and Lucy (Paschal) Berry, had a son, James H. Berry. (*Berry)

written enough stuff for this time, so no more at present.
Yours With Respect, A. N. Pachal. P S Write as soon as you
get this and take care of Old Blacks colt.

Undated partial letter:

. . . and gather a few and put sugar and cream on them but
I am not their. I hope that you may have the pleasure of
gathering a portion of them. When you go out their take
Blake along. He might find another turkeys nest. I have been
getting all of the dewberies that I wanted for some time but
they are almost gone. They were very nice. We get plenty
of sugar and it is just the thing for that sort of fruit. A little
cream would be very nice but that is one of the articles that
souldiers has to do without. When you write again, I want
you to tell me how the girls are getting along in that neighbor-
hood. Girls down here are very scarce but their are plenty of
young men and old batchelors and the most of them say they
intend to get married shortly after they return home. It would
do you good to see our camp [and] to see the tents and the
men doing their own cooking and washing. They saw pork
barrels in two for tubs, make wooden washboards [and the]
goverment furnishes the soap. This country is left to grow up
in weeds this season. The farmers has all left. Some planta-
tions have a few darkies left upon them. They are a farming
for them selves to raise something to live on. Their are several
places in the south that they are a farming pretty largely but I
think that we will stop their supplies from Texas this summer.
That is our greatest hope to stop the rebellion. If we can get the
Mississippi River clear I think we will have their Southeren
Confederacy divided into two parts and then we can whip
half of it at a time. I reckon the farmers up north is a pitching
in just like there was no war a going on in the country. They
would feel kinder funny if about the time they got their crops

*in that their would come a draft and take them away from
their plows and their corn fields but I hope this will not be the
case. So no more at present. From your Brother, A. N. Paschal
P.S. In this letter I will send a ten dollar green back. Answer
soon. Give my respects to all. Tell Will that I got them stamps
and will answer his letter soon.*

Undated partial letter:

*I would like to be up their to help you plant corn about this
time I havent saw any thing planted down here yet. The corn
that come up by chance that has got scattered around is three
feet high. The weeds that come up on the farms this spring are
as high as my head. Their are plenty of alagators down here.
They are no show at all to me. This is the greatest country
for varments ever I got into. Their is most any thing that you
could mention but White Folks, with the exceptions of the
souldiers. The whites had all left this part of the country and
Uncle Sam is a going to take the darkies. Their is being Negro
Regiments made up in their section to fight the Rebels that
is scouting around the country in gurillar bands. They are to
have white officers. Our orderly is to be captain of a Company
of them. I think it will suit him very well. Orange Sacket[106]
wanted [to be] an officer but they did not take but one out
of a Company so he was sadly disapointed. I believe I have
writen enough for this time, so no more. Yours with respect A
N Paschal PS. Write as soon as you get this and dont forget to
send a stamp or two and you will oblige me very much. Give
my respects to all inquiring friends. PS. Is Old Blacks colt a
horse or a mair?*

---

106 Orange E. Sackett (114th Ill, Co. A) was mustered out August 3, 1865, with the rank of corporal. (*Sackett). The orderly that Newton refers to is probably Sergeant Norman S. Hitchcock of Beardstown who became the 1st Lieutenant of Company K, 71st U.S. Colored Troops.

Warren Co Missisppi, Camp eight miles from Vicksburg, June 18,

Dear Sister: It is with pleasure I resume my seat to answer yours of June the 5. I was very glad to hear from you all and that you were well. I am well and hearty. I havent nothing of any importance to communicate to you at present. The seige is still kept at Vicksburg. We are still wating for Johnson[107] and his army but they appear to be kinder shy or dont care much about pitching in but I would not wonder if they came around and give us a call one of these days. If they do come we will give them the best we have in the shop. Vicksburg holds out wonderfuly but we have no reasons to doubt but what she will fall before long for it would be almost imposable for them to do other wise. The weather has been a little cooler for the last few days with showers of rain. I was out a picking blackberies to day and found two bee trees. I expect to cut them tomorow. I heard this morning that Will Crow had got back home. I hope it may be true. Our Company is in better health than it has been for some time. Apples and peaches are commencing to get ripe in about a month. I wish I could send you some of our southern fruit for I think it would be quite a rarity to you. I was sorry to hear that Cousin Joe Street[108] was in the hospital. I wish you would give me the name of his Co and regiment for I would like to write to him. You spoke of the girls all being unionests. I hope they may keep in that notion until I return home. I think their will be some chance for me although I am a getting to be quite an old bachelor. But I dont think they will have mutch the advantage of me for they are growing in years as well as my self. I expect the Miss Dunns[109] makes good school teachers. Tell

---

107 Newton is misspelling the name of Major General Joseph E. Johnston, commander of all Confederate forces between the Appalachian Mts. and the Mississippi River during the Battle of Vicksburg.

108 Joseph E. Street (19th Iowa Infantry, Company E) enlisted in Lee Co., Iowa. (*Street)

109 Emlin Dunn and Mary Ann Dunn were sisters and apparently teaching school. (*Dunn)

them they must not whip the small schollars but make the large ones toe the mark. Tell them that I would be very glad to hear from them and how they enjoy school teaching. Tell Mary I realy would like to be at home a few days just to see how the people looks but I have no time to be there but I hope the time is not far distant. Darwin Lindsley is with the Co again. H. Freeman & James Berry are both well. I get to see some of the sesesh girls now adays but I havent fell in love with any of them yet. Some of them are very good looking but they think a little to mutch of Jeff Davis for me. I believe they are stronger sesesh than their men but they ant quite so dangerous. It appears that brother Joe and Will Crow beet me back home. I think the next time I start with them any where I will make them promise to go all the way before I start. I reckon I will have to excuse them this time for they was mutch longer. I was glad to hear that greenback got home safe. I believe I have wrote enough of foolishness for this time. Write soon, so no more at present. Yours truly. A.N. Paschal

Warren County, Mississippi, June 29, 1863

Dear Brother: It is with pleaure I take my pen to answer your letter of June the 15th. I was very glad to hear from you but I think you forgot to mention how the rest of the folks were a getting along but I reckon their wasent any of them sick or you would of mentioned them. I am well and enjoying myself fine. We are now about 14 miles from Vicksburg as usual but they havent taken the city yet. I dont think they can hold out mutch longer for their provisions must be very near exhausted by this time. I havent any news of any impotence for I havent read a news paper lately. The weather is very warm and dry. We are encamped clost to good spring watter and a good blackberry patch. Fruit is very plenty out here. The boys appear to be enjoying them selves very well and they are tollerable healthy.

They appear to have got over the most of their home sickness. I am fleshier now than I have been since I left Illinois and lazy enough but I think if I was up there I could make my hand in the harvest field if they would give me plenty of grubb. I expect that it would go pretty hard with me to work a little now after doing nothing so long. It wont be a great while now until one third of my time will be up. Will be mustered for pay tomorow but I dont know when the paymaster will be around but I expect it wont be a great while. The news down here is that the Copperheads are a getting pretty thick up north and intend to resist the draft but I hardly think it is true. If they do their will just be a little more fighting for us to do thats all. We have got a few negr o regiments to put against them that I think would give them some fun at any rate. I would like to be with you up to the fair but I hardly think I will unless things takes a considrable change. I expect that I will have to stay where I am needed the most this summer. If the war would end then I might talk about fairs and the like but it is no use for me to bother my self about sutch things now, for a little county fair wouldnt be no show at all to me now for I have seen more curiosities since I left home than it would take to fill up Barnums Show[110] and then have two or three side shows to boot. It would be more of a show now for me to see my relatives than anything else or some bodies girl or something of that kind. I have got to commence cooking my dinner so I will stop writing for this time.

Yours with respect, A. N. Paschal

PS. I will send a five dollar greenback in this letter and you can give it to Mary and she will know where to stow it away. Write soon and give me all the news that you pick up for you can see by this letter that I have about run out of news myself.

---

110 Phineas T. Barnum started his tent shows of "curiosities" in 1836 and opened his famous American Museum in New York City in 1842. The Museum burned in 1868. The well-known traveling shows did not begin until 1871.

Warren County, Mississippi, July 1, 1863

Dear Brother [Will]: It is with pleasure I take my pen to write you a few lines. I am well. I wrote you a letter day before yesterday and sent $5 in it. We was payed two months pay yesterday and I expressed twenty dollars to James B. Leonards[111] Bank, Beardstown, to you. I expect it will get there just about as soon as this letter. I would be very mutch obliged if you would go and get it and give it to sister Mary and tell her to put it on interest the first good oppertunity. I havent anything of any importance to write at present. We are still a waiting for the Rebels to come in this way. They are always comeing but dont get their. Was a few got on this side of the Black River day before yesterday but they got back some quicker than they came over. Our guns are still playing on Vicksburg. Our men intend to show them how mutch noise they can make on the fourth. Their was a man died in our Co. yesterday with the intermitant fever by the name of John Jefferson[112]. He belonged to my mess but he hasent been with us mutch lately. He has been cooking over the fire. This hot weather was the cause of his death. The weather is very warm and dry but we have some very nice shade trees at this camp and I enjoy myself very well in the shade. We dont have mutch to do except cook and eat and lay in the shade and answer to roll call. I heard that the Copperheads had a very large meeting at Springfield but I havent got the particulars of their meeting yet. I expect they had a fine time up there. I would of liked to of been there to hear then spout, for I would like to know whether they intend to resist the draft or not. I think if I had of been there I could of formed a pretty good idea of their intentions but I dont expect they are very dangerous any way. The cannons are fireing very briskly at Vicksburg this

---

111 James B. Leonard, born in 1818 in New Jersey, owned the bank in Beardstown, Cass County, Illinois.

112 John Jefferson, of Fulton County, Illinois, died in the field on June 30, 1863.

morning. I think their is something more than common going on there. Perhaps the Rebells is trying to break out again. They undertook that trick last week and got about a thousand of thier men killed at the process. Our loss in repulsing them was about five hundred killed wounded and prisnors. I havent heard from Hooker's army or Rosencrans lately but I dont expect they are idle. So no more at present. Write soon and send me twenty five cents worth of stamps. Yours with respect, A. N. Paschal

When it became apparent that Johnston would not come to the rescue, General John Pemberton took the advice of his staff and surrendered to Grant. It was perhaps the most important Union victory of the Civil War. It brought great fame to both Grant and Sherman. Realizing that he had finally found a general who would fight, President Abraham Lincoln would turn to Grant to finish the war.

Photograph by Joe Fulton.

The beautiful memorial to Illinois soldiers at the Vicksburg National Military Park. Many of the names of soldiers mentioned in this book are engraved on the walls of this stunning monument, including the names of Asa Newton Paschal and Henry Freeman.

Ironically, at the time of the surrender of Vicksburg, the Union army was also engaged in what would become the most famous battle of the Civil War: Gettysburg. In yet another twist of historic irony, Pemberton surrendered Vicksburg on the 4th of July. The vanquished people of Vicksburg responded by refusing to celebrate Independence Day for the next 100 years.

Following the fall of Vicksburg, the men of the 114th remained encamped along the Big Black River. They were part of the force that would chase Johnston further away from the city he never reached. They pursued him as far a Brandon, a few miles east of Jackson, before being recalled by Sherman. They would remain in Warren County, Mississippi until November. For most of that time they were at "Camp Sherman" along the Big Black which Newton described as "one of the nicest camps in the south."

Newton remarks with pride in a letter dated Sept. 17th that Brigadier General Ralph Buckland had selected Co. A of the 114th to receive horses and serve as scouts for the entire brigade.

In several of the letters that follow Newton attacks the Copperheads with as much venom as he had attacked the abolitionists. The Copperheads, or Peace Democrats, was a splinter group of the northern Democratic Party that opposed the war and/or supported the sovereignty of the South. The name Copperheads arose because many of the Peace Democrats wore identifying copper pins on their lapels. The most noted leader of the Copperheads was Clement L. Vallandigham of Ohio.

Photograph by Joe Fulton.

A marker at the Vicksburg National Military Park honoring the men of the 114th Illinois.

Camp Near Black River, July 27, 1863

*Dear Sister [Mary]: It is with pleasure I take my pen in hand
to answer you kind letter of July the fifth which I received day
before yesterday. It found me well and hearty but considerbly
fatighued with marching. I have been in a fight or two but
I got through safe. We crost the Black River July the 6 and
followed Johnson's army to Jackson where he stopped and had
us a battle.[113] We fought about six days and we were about
getting the better of him when he evacuated the town. He fell
back in the direction of Mobile and part of his forses stoped
at a little town by the name of Brandon twelve miles from
Jackson on the railroad and we marched out there and had a
nice little battle. Our loss was one killed. The rebels was about
thirty killed and wounded. Our loss at Jackson was about 4
hundred killed and wounded. The Rebels loss was greater than
ours. We took about two thousand prisnors and they only took
about sixty of our men. The greater part of the prisnors that
we took laid down their arms and came in to our lines and
gave themselves up. They say that they are tired of the war
and wont fight any more. The sesesh army has about played
out in this section of the Confedracy. Old Johnson's army is
scattered so that it will take him a long time to get it together
again if he can do it at all. Our Reg crost the Black River on
our return from Jackson day before yeterday. We will be apt
to camp not far about for some time probably for a month
or 2. This is the first letter I have writen since the fifth of July
and it is the first opportunity that I have had. Their was six
wounded in our Reg at Jackson and three of them belonged to*

---

113 "The Regiment was ordered to move against the Rebel General, Joe Johnston, who
retreated to Jackson, Miss.--during the siege of which place the loss of the Regiment, in killed and wounded, was 7 men. Johnston evacuating, it followed him as
far as Brandon, and then returned to Camp Sherman, near Vicksburg." Adjutant
General's Report.

*Co A, John Wedeking[114], Schmehl[115] & F. Unland[116]. Wedeking
had his right leg amputated. Unland slight wound in left arm.
Schmehl foot in the heel. Their are being some furlows granted
but the married men will get to go home first and they ought
to. I would like to see you all very well but I dont expect to pay
you a visit until next spring unless the war closes. Their will
be three start home on furlows in a day or two R. F. Kippenberg[117], Amos Adkins[118], Snider[119] or a Dutchman, I dont know
which. It is not desided yet. You wanted to know if I knew
anything of T Cuppy. I do not. I never saw him at Memphis
but I saw some of his Co and they said that he was left on a
boat sick and they expected that he would be sent to St. Louis.
I saw Will Garlick[120] the other day and also Thos Ayers[121] of
Beardstown. Old Mr Sacket arrived here yesterday and two
other old gentlemen with relation in other companies. As I
have no convenient place of writing I will quit for this time. I
sat down on a log and held this on my knee while I wrote it.
Write soon. Yours with respect, A. N. Paschal*

*PS. Tell Will I will write to him in a few days. Tell Grub that I
sent 20 dollars to Leonards Bank Beardstown some time ago
and would like to know whether he got it or not.*

---

114 John H. Weddeking enlisted on August 4, 1862, but because of his wounds was absent from muster out on August 3, 1865. (*Weddeking)

115 Conrad Schmehl enlisted on August 13, 1862, but because of wounds was absent at muster out on August 3, 1865. (*Schmehl)

116 George Frederick Unland enlisted August 11, 1862, and transferred to Veterans Reserve Corps on September 30, 1864. (*Unland)

117 Richard F. Kippenberg (114th Ill, Co. A) was mustered out June 22, 1865. (*Kippenberg)

118 Amos D. Adkins (114th Ill, Co. A) was mustered out June 5, 1865. (*Adkins)

119 Uriah Snyder (114th Ill, Co. A) was mustered out August 3, 1865. (*Snyder)

120 William B. Garlick (*Garlick)

121 Thomas Ayers (*Ayers)

Camp near Black River, July 31, 1863

Dear Brother [Will]: I take my pen to answer your letter of July the 5. I was glad to hear you were all well. I am well at present and hope this may find you all the same. I have done considrable marching since I last wrote to you and have had the pleasure of shooting at the Rebels but we are now in camp enjoying ourselves at the best advantage. The weather is very warm and sultry. We have had considerable rain within the last week and looks very mutch like rain this morning. I do not know how long we will stay at this camp but I hope we will stay until the weather gets a little cooler. I think our next move will be down the river to Natches or Mobile. We have got the rebels about cleaned out in this section of the country. It will soon be twelve months since I enlisted and I have seen just about as mutch of the Southern Confedracy as I care about seeing in that length of time. I would like to be up in Illinois a while and see you all but I dont know whether I will pay you a visit before my time is out or not. I would not give two cents for a furlow for I dont think that it would be any pleasure to me to come home and stay two or three days and then have to pack up my duds and start back. I am of the opinion that when a calf is about half weaned it is best for it to stay away from its mother. Besides it would cost something to go and come and I dont know as I have any buisness at home only to see and be seen. Their are several in the Co that has business at home and I think that they are the ones that ought to go. You said that you had been enrolled. I expect you would make a pretty good souldier but I hope you will not be drafted for then Old Blake will be left alone with Mother. I havent any idea how long this war will last yet but I have about made up my mind to souldier out my three years. Their has been considerable fighting down about Charleston lately but I havent heard the particulars yet. Our army is in better spirits than it was last spring but it is considerable worn out [from] heavy marching and fatague. If we get about a months rest I think it will recruit up again. We are encamped clost to some nice springs of splended water and under good shade trees which suits me very well you bet. I havent got any letters lately from anyone and if I dont get some pretty soon I am a going to quit writing my self. I wrote Mary a letter three or four days ago. I am about out of stamps but I have plenty of paper & envelops but I cant find any stamps that I can bye and I dont like to send letters without stamps for I dont think they are as apt to go through. I would like to know how the copperheads takes it about the fall of Vicksburg and surrounding country. You can tell them that Jackson, Miss burnt to ashes. The only way that you can tell that their was a city is by the ashes and old brick walls and other rubush that wouldent burn. The railroads and depoes are also torn up and burned in that vicinity and if this army that is hear should ever be ordered to South Carolina their wont be enough of that place left to tell it was a state. I expect we will be down there in less than six months from now if the sesesh feels inclined to keep up the war so long. Small squads of Rebs are still comeing into our lines and taking paroles and going home. They say that they are tired of the war and dont intend to fight. This sheet is so poor that I cant write only two pages of it. We will be payed off again in a few days and I expect to send a portion of it home by some of the boys that goes to Illinois on furlows. I believe that I have writen enough, so no more at present. Yours, A. N. Paschal PS. Write soon and give me the news for I havent any to write but I have sent to Vicksburg for a newspaper and expect to be posted up in a few days.

Camp Near Black River, August 2, 1863

Dear Sister [Mary]: It is with pleasure I take my pen to write you a few lines to let you know that I am well and hope this will find you all the same. I havent any news of any importance to write but as I have an opertunity of sending this with a friend. He has got a furlow and is about on the point of starting home. Their are also two others of the Co comeing home, Amos D. Adkin s & Henry Gestring[122]. I sent fifteen dollars to Will by Gestring in the care of Ira Crow. Will send you ten dollars in this letter. I sent twenty dollars by express sometime ago to Leonards Bank in Wills name. I would like to know whether he got it or not. I will be payed two months wages this week. I wish I had it now while I have a chance of sending it home. The last letter that I have received from any of you was dated July the 5 and I am a getting a little uneasy about affairs at home for I think that I ought to of had another letter before this time. Our Army in this section of the country are all in the camp and I think we will stay here for some time. We are a going to send to Vicksburg tomorow for our tents. Our Regiment hasent had any tents to sleep in since the first of last May. I expect we will be quite at home when we get in tents again. The weather still continues very warm with frequent showers. I went out this evening and gathered a sack of peaches. I intend to make a cobler tomorow. We will have plenty of sweet potatoes soon but their are so many troops around here I expect that things will soon be getting scarse for souldiers all likes nicknacks. I wrote Grub a letter day before yesterday and you one or two days before that. I havent any news from below. I saw in a St Louis Paper that Morgan's[123] forces had been smashed up and captured. I havent any news

---

122 Henry C. Gestring (114th Ill, Co. A) of Cass County, Illinois, was taken prisoner at Guntown, Mississippi and died of his wounds on June 17, 1864.

123 Brig. Gen. James D. Morgan (1810-1896), native of Massachusetts, was commander of the Army of the Cumberland, 2nd Division, Reserve Corps, at the time of this letter. He led brigades at Island No. 10 and Corinth.

of the Army of the Potomack. I would like to be at the Cass County Fair but I believe I shant take the trouble of going to it this season. I want you to tell my relations that I would like to see them all very mutch but I dont expect to see them until the war is over. If we should move any farther south which I think in all probablilty we will this fall if the war dont wind up soon. We all feel very greatful over the victories that we have gained over our oponents in the last month or two and I think we ought to for what we have went through and dangers enough to earn all we have gained. I hope we will still keep on gaining victory after victory until their can [be peace] all over the land for I think this war has been kept up long enough, not altogether on my account but for the welfare of our country. So no more tonight. Yours with respect. A.N. Paschal PS. Write soon and send me the news I would like for you to let me know how mutch money I have sent home since I enlisted for I havent kept any account of it at all. Give my love to all inquiring friends and to the girls especily. If the draft comes off in that section I want you to let me know who is drafted in that neighborhood.

Camp near Black River, August 9, 1863

Dear Brother [Will]: It is with mutch pleasure I sit down to write you a few lines in answer to yours of the twenty ninth which I was very glad to receive and that you were all well with the exception of Mary which I was very sorry to hear was unwell but I hope she will soon recover as you said she was better. I am well and hope this will find you all the same. I havent anything of importance to write at this time. We are in Camp and their is no signs of us moveing any ways soon. I calculate to send this letter by Major McLane[124] as he is going

---

124 Major Joseph M. McLane (114th Ill, Co. A). (*McLane)

*to start home day after tomorrow on a furlow and he told me
if I would write he would take my letters to Beardstown for me
with pleasure which I thank him for his kindness very mutch.
James Berry, H. Freeman, Thos. Brown and all of the boys
that you are acquainted with are well. Berry has been sick but
he looks tollerable well now. The weather is very warm and
sweltry. I was very glad to hear that their had been rain in that
section of the country which you must been in great need of
after such a long drouth but it must have been very provoking
to get your linen wet as you did upon that day but if you was
in the army you would soon get ust to getting wet. I have been
out in pretty near [everything] that we have had this summer
but we have got our tents now and have got one of the nicest
camps in the south. Recon we sweep all over every day regular
and keep every thing clean and nice. When them other boys
went home I sent fifteen dollars by Gestring in care of Ira Crow
and ten by Kippenburg to Joe in a letter directed to you. I was
very glad to learn that money got through safe I sent some
time ago being as I have been paid of lately and am not coming
home any ways soon and dont have mutch use for money at
present. I will send twenty dollars in this and keep six for to bye
notions with sutch as cigars and tobacco. I supose you enjoyed
your selves hugely up at Clear Lake[125] on the fourth of July but
you did not say whether you danced or not. But I am rather
inclined to think you did as you ust to like the sport. I hope you
may have a good time a huckstering. I only have a few more
days to souldier and then one third of my time will be up and
I am not very sorry that it is. Grub I would like you to get that
note, that of mine on Wm Crow and tell Crow that if he is tired
of paying interest on it he can have a chance of paying it off. I
dont know whether Mary has the note or Ira Crow but you can*

---

125 This is probably the small lake in Cass County about five miles northeast of Beardstown. The lake on which Camp Butler, east of Springfield, Illinois, is built, is also
known as Clear Lake, but, since this would be some distance for them to travel for
a 4th of July celebration, it is probably the one near Beardstown.

easily find out by enquiring. I will quit writing for this time. Write soon and give me the news. So no more to knight. Yours with repect, A.N. Paschal to Wm.

Camp near Black River, August 28, 1863

Dear Sister [Mary]: It is with pleasure I resume my pen this morning to answer your kind letter of Aug the 14th which I received yesterday evening. I was exceeding glad to hear from you but was sory to hear that yourself and Mother was unwell but I hope that you both are well before this arrives. I am well at present and hope this will find you all the same. Our Co is in tollarable good health. We are still in our camp and I havent seen any indications of moveing anyways soon. Fruit of all kinds has about played in this section of the country. I reckon we will have to do without fruit until we move from this Camp. I havent any important news of any kind. Ft. Sumpter is reported tore to atoms but it is not confirmed. We get St Louis papers here regular at the small sum of fifteen cts a piece and Harpers Weekly for twenty five cents. They are generaly about four days old when we get them. The time for the boys that went home has almost expired. I do not know whether any more will go home or not when they return. If they do it will be Milton McLane[126], Victor J. Philippi[127] & Jacob Stuckey[128]. We drew for furloughs in our Co yesterday and I drew a blank but I did not care any great deal for I did not care mutch for I did not want to come home at present any way, and their was lots that did. I would like to be with Will a peddling melones but I dont think it would be any great satisfaction for me to come home and stay a few days and

---

126 Joseph Milton McLane (1st Lieut, 114th Ill, Co. A), son of Major Joseph M. McLane. (*McLane)

127 Victor J. Phillippi (Sergeant, 114th Ill, Co. A), was mustered out on May 28, 1865. (*Phillippi)

128 Jacob S. Stuckey (114th Ill, Co. A) (*Stuckey)

come back down south. I think this war will close before a great
while any way and if it does I will then get the kind of a furlough
that will be some account. But if this war should go on a year
longer I expect to come home in that time. I will come home
about Christmas if I can get a furlough if the war should last so
long. The weather has been some cooler for the past week and is
nice and cool to day. I thank you very mutch for that list. When
I came to look over the list I found out that I had sent home
more money than I thought. I sent twenty dollars by the Major.
I expect you have got it before this. I will give you a few prices of
a few articles in our camp. Butter 50 cents, dried peaches 25cts
per lb, apples 20cts per lb, cucumber pickles 5 cts a piece and
other things according. It appears that you dont write very often
or anybodie else. Your letter is the only one that I have recieved
in about a month. I want you to be very particular in directing
your letters, especily the Co and Reg for their are so many
careless post masters. If letters aint marked very plane they
are very apt to go astray and when a letter gets into the wrong
regiment it is generly broken open and sometimes distroyed. It
is about time for the Cass County Fair to be comeing off I hope
they will have a fine time and that you will be able to go. Henry
Freeman and James Berry are well. Darwin Lindsley aint any
account for a souldier but if he was at home I think he would do
to farm. He is always on the sick list. I have made considrable
inquiry about Thomas Cuppy but havent heard of him. I wrote
Joe Street a letter but havent got any answer yet. Write soon,
so no more at present. Your Brother, A. N. Paschal PS. Give my
respects to all and especialy girls of that neighborhood.

Oak Ridge, Mississippi, September 6, 1863

*Dear Brother [Will]: It is with pleasure I take my pen to write
you a few lines to let you know that I am well and hope this will
find you all the same. I havent received any letters from you*

for some time. The last letter I recieved was from Mary dated August the 14th. I have got tired of waiting for a letter from you and come to the conclusion that I would send you one. We have moved from our old camp about six miles[129]. We havent quite as nice a camp ground as we had but we have plenty of good water. Kippenburg and Gestring has got back from Illinois but Adkins hasent got back yet. It is a getting tollerable sticky down here. The weather has been for the past week but the nights are getting cool and a fellow can sleep to a pretty good advantage. Their is nothing going on in this section worth mentioning at present. Their is a report in Camp today that Charleston is taken but it is not certain yet but such a thing might be possible. Grub, I have got a niger wench to do my cooking. We have got six niger cooks in the Company. We have considrable picket duty to do at this Camp but I had just about as soon stand picket as lay around Camp. Their hasent been any more of the boys started home on furlows yet. Their cant any more start until them gets back that went last month and their isnt over half of them back yet. Their hasent been [Remainder of letter lost]

Oak Ridge, Mississippi, September 15, 1863

It is very warm this morning. Their are no news of note in camp this morning. Their is to be sixty men out of our Brigade mounted on horse back for scouts. They are to be commanded by our Captain so our Company will be commanded by Lieut. McClure[130] for a while. The object of this scouting party is to

---

129 "Ordered to Oak Ridge, Miss., and, while doing picket duty there, had several skirmishes with guerrillas. Lieutenant McClure, Company A, was killed, and 2 men captured, while on duty. While there the Regiment participated in two scouts." Adjutant General's Report

130 Joseph A. McClure (114th Ill, Co. A), was born in 1840, the son of Joseph and Ruth McClure. He had been a schoolteacher before he enlisted on September 18, 1862. He was killed during a skirmish at Oak Ridge, Mississippi on October 2, 1863.

pick up small squads of rebels that is roaming around through the country. I was talking with a sesesh girl the other night and ast her what she thought of the Copperheads up north and she said that she thought that they all deserved hanging. She considered them cowards and traitors. She said that she thought more of the Union souldiers than she did of them for they come out and show what they are but the Copperheads are at home a doing no good either for the north or south. She says that the rebel souldiers calls them the drones of the army and it would be better if they were killed off for sutch cowards as them ought not to be let live in or disgrace this continent by their cowardly conduct. She says if the south should gain their independance they could never put any dependence in the Copperheads for a people acting as they are will never do to trust. General Gillmore[131] is still a operating with his men about Charlestown and it is our sincere hope and belief that he will take that place before long but the weather is so hot that we cant expect to hear of an attack at the present. But it will soon be time for the weather to get cooler and then I think their will be a general move on the rebel works throughout the south and if we are sucsessful I think that the rebellion will soon be wound up or wore out just as you are a mind to call it. But war is a uncertain thing and wont do to bet on. I do not know how mutch longer we will stay at this camp but I hope that we will stay until the weather gets cooler for I aint very fond of marching in hot weather. I believe I will bring this letter to a close. You must excuse me for not writing more when you are so kind as to furnish the paper and stamps. Write soon, so no more at present.

Yours with respect, A. N. Paschal

Give my love to all inquiring friends and relations and to the girls of that neighborhood.

---

131 Brig. Gen. Quincy Adams Gillmore (1825-1888), native of Ohio, Commander of the 10th Corps, Department of the South, had begun expeditions against Charleston on September 8.

Oak Ridge, Mississippi, September 16, 1863

Dear Sister [Mary]: It is with pleasure I take my pen to answer your kind letter of August the 28th which I was glad to get for I was ancious to hear how Mother is. I was very sorry to hear of the death of little Grace[132] but was glad to hear the rest of the family was in tollerble health. I am well and hope this will find you all the same. The Major got back day before yesterday and brought me four letters. The weather is very warm at present down here and has been for some time but I dont think it is quite as stickly as it has been for some time past. I havent anything of any importance to write at present. We are almost doing nothing now adays. I havent any news worth mentioning of other parts of the army. I heard that their had been some fighting done on the other side of the Mississippi River near Little Rock. I am sorry that the Copperheads are getting so numerous up there but I think that their are Union men enough left to hold them strait. If I was up there I would be apt to make some of them smell gun powder if they did not stop their tongues for I consider them the worst enimies that the Union has got to contend with. I am still in favor of the Union as I ever have been and have no idea of deserting it in its time of trouble. I heard that W. Crow had left home again. It looks like his discharge wasent of the right stripe.[133] I have come to the conclusion that he has took a French leave[134] and cant well stay in Beardstown. It is a pity that he has thrown himself away in this kind of stile. Well Mary I would like to come home but I dont think that I will ever get there if I have to get there by desertion for I still

---

132 No record survives to tell us about Grace. Perhaps she was an infant child of Newton's brother Joseph Paschal who was married to Mary Crow.

133 Adjutant General's Report indicates that William F. Crow deserted on June 29, 1863.

134 French leave is defined as "an 18th century French custom of leaving a reception without taking leave of the host or hostess; an informal, hasty, or secret departure." Webster's New Collegiate Dictionary, 1975.

think that their will be a time that I can get out of the army honerably and I do not think the time is far distant for I do not think the war can last always. The boys in Co. A are well. Milton McLane is gone home on a furlow. I was out to see a sesesh girl the other nite and had quite a chat with her. Their was a souldier on an Iowa Reggot married to a young lady down here a few days ago, so you can see the sesesh girls like the Union Boys pretty well. I dont know but what I might take a fancy to some of them yet to what I know. I hardly think I will although their are some very good looking ones around here. But I am afeard they dont know how to work and I think they would hardly suit me. [Remainder of letter lost]

Oak Ridge, Mississippi, September 17, 1863

Dear Brother: It is with pleasure I take my pen to answer your kind letter of August the thirtieth. I was glad to hear from you and that you were well. I am well and hearty and hope this will find you the same. Our Co. is to be mounted and Co E also to act as scouts around here. Capt. Johnson[135] has command of the two companies. We will still stay with the Reg and act as scouts for our Brigade. Our Company was chosen by the Brigadier General out of the whole Brigade. I think that I will enjoy the business very well and get a few chickens to eat out in the country. We will get our horses today or tomorrow. Their are very good news from Arkansas and Steele's[136] & Blunt's[137] men. They have taken Little Rock and whipped the

---

135 John M. Johnson (114th Ill, Co. A) was promoted to Major on September 18, 1862. He was mustered out on August 3, 1865.

136 Maj. Gen. Frederick Steele (1819-1868), from New York, was commanding the Arkansas Expedition, Army of the Tennessee, at the time of this letter.

137 Brig. Gen. James G. Blunt (1826-1881), native of Maine, was commanding District of the Frontier, Department of Missouri, at the time of this letter.

rebels most beautifully out in that section of the Country.[138]
Their is no news from below worth mentioning. I fear Gilmore
is not getting along as well as has been antisipated but I think
that he will hang and keep fighting until he reduces them
rebel forts and yet march into Charleston. All is quiet on the
Potomac. At this account Rosencrans is in the neighborhood
of Chattanooga[139] *and we are expecting every day to hear*
of him doing some hard fighting. The Rebs are a pressing in
every thing that they can make a souldier out of. They are
now putting arms into the hands of the negroes and compel-
ling them to fight. Their was ten negroes came up to our picket
last night and the pickets halted them. They thought that our
men was rebs and they turned around when our pickets fired
on them and killed one and shot another through the foot
but they came inside of our lines this morning. I was detailed
yesterday to go and get some horses before I got through
writing this letter so I will finish it today. We got horses and
saddles yesterday for our Co and we went out with General
Bucklin[140] *to the Yazoo River bottom the distance of eight miles*
from Camp. I do not expect we will be in Camp mutch of our
time for a spell so I dont expect that I will write very regular.
But I will write when I have an opportunity and I want you to
do the same. I think that I will like souldiering on horseback
very well but I expect that I will have more work to do. But
I think that I can take care of one horse without grumbling
a great deal. We had a very nice rain yesterday and to day is
very cool and pleasant and looks a little like the fall of the year.

---

138 On September 10, Little Rock, Arkansas, an important Confederate center, which had been under attack by Frederick Steele's expedition moving from Helena, Arkansas, was evacuated by Southern forces.

139 On September 16, Rosecrans was concentrating his Army of the Cumberland in the area of Lee and Gordon's Mills on Chickamauga Creek, Georgia, about 12 miles south of Chattanooga.

140 Brig. Gen. Ralph P. Buckland (1812-1892), native of Massachusetts, was commanding the 1st Brigade, 1st Division, 16th Corps, Army of the Tennessee, at the time of this letter.

I am very sorry that it has been so cool up north for it must of put a damper on your watermelon melon trade and I expect the frost has done considerable damage to crops in Illinois. I never heard of so heavy a frost in August before. I believe I have writen all that I can think of at present. Write soon again and give me the news. Yours with respect, A. N. Paschal

Oak Ridge, Mississippi, September 21, 1863

To Samuel T. Paschal: Well, Blake, I am a going to write you a few lines to let you know that I havent forgotten you and to let you know that I am well and hearty and hope this will find you all the same. I hardly know what to write that would interest you. Well Tom I have got a horse to ride now adays instead of traveling a foot. The horse that I have got is a little sorrel and he can out run any of the rest in the Company. We was out on scout yesterday about twenty five miles from Camp. We run on to a squad of guerillars and they broke and run into the woods and brush. We run our horses up to the brush and got off of them. Part of us stoped to hold the horses and the rest of us run in to the woods after them but they all made their escape except one and we took him and brought him in camp. He was armed with a revoler and a double barrel shot gun. The weather is nice and cool and has been for three or four days. We get plenty of peaches and sweet potatoes when we are out in the country. Blake, I want you to take out any old shot gun and practice shooting ducks, geese and all of the dogs that you dont like. I want you to do all of the devilment that you can to them Copperheads up there. You bet they would catch us if I was up there for I think they are a cowardly low lifed set at best and it would do me good to devill them all I could. I would like to see you all very well but I am a getting kinder weaned from Illinois and if I was to come back I would be a sucker again and you know that a calf is hard to wean when it gets about half weaned and gets back to the cow. The latest news is that Gen. Gilmore has got possesion of the whole of Morris Island, Ft. Wagner, Gregg and all and is giving Ft. Sumter fits.[141] *Blake their are lots of sesesh girls down here about your age and some that is good looking. I am a going out with some teams in the morning to get corn for our horses. We use the rebels corn and save Uncle Sam the trouble of furnishing feed. You must write soon, so no more at present. From your brother, A.N. Paschal*

Oak, Ridge, Mississippi, September 27, 1863

Dear Brother & Sister: It is with pleasure I sit down to answer your kind letter of Sept the thirteenth. I was very glad to hear from you and that you and the rest of the family were well. I am well and the health of the boys is generly good. I havent anything of any importance to write at present. We was out on a scout yesterday and saw eight guirillars and fired a few shots at them and wounded one and got one of their horses. I expect that we will go out again this evening. Our Division has been detached to the Seventeenth Army Corps and the Fifteenth Army Corps commanded by Sherman is under marching orders. It is supposed they are a going to reinforce Rosecrans. General Tuttle[142] *has again taken command of our division and I expect he will be Commander of the post at Vicksburg. If he is we will be apt to winter in Vicksburg this winter. We havent any news from Charleston or other places worth mentioning. I was very sorry to hear that the Rebs had taken Mr. Richard but I hope they will treat him well. We get*

---

141 During the night of September 6-7, the Confederate garrisons of Fort Wagner on Charleston's Morris Island and Fort Gregg, beseiged since early July, were evacuated. Fort Sumter held out despite its almost total destruction.

142 Brig. Gen. James Madison Tuttle (1823-1892), native of Ohio, was commnading the 3rd Division, 15th Corps, Army of the Tennessee, at the time of this letter.

plenty of peaches and sweet potatoes out in the country and sometimes we get milk and butter. I got all the milk that I could drink yesterday. You spoke of Will a getting a letter from Cousin Boots[143]. I wrote a letter to Boots about two months ago but he hasent answered it yet. I reckon he must of a made a mistake and wrote to Grub instead of me. I hope you enjoyed yourselves at the fair but I expect their was plenty of mud after the rain around the fair ground. I expect that their was lots of pretty girls thare and if I could of been thare I would of asisted in leading them around. I got a letter from a girl day before yesterday that lives in Illinois but I havent answered it yet for I havent had time. Tommy said that Grub started down the fence while he was a writing and expected that he would climb over the fence and strike acrost the farm before he went far. I suppose by that he makes a practice of going down to Dunns yet for that is the way he ust to go before I left home. I would like to know which of the girls he goes to see for I think that he has been going thare long enough to get one of them.[144] I am a feard that he will be an old batch yet if he dont hurry up. So no more at present. A. N. Paschal PS. Write soon. I wrote Blake a letter three or four days ago. You must excuse bad wrting for it was done in haste. ANP

Warren County, Mississippi, November 3, 1863

Dear Brother: It is with pleasure I take my pen to answer your kind letter of Oct the eleventh. I was glad to hear from you and that you were well but was sorry that Mothers health was so poor this fall. My health is very good and I hope this will find you all enjoying the same. I have nothing of any importance to

---

143 This is probably Joseph Street to whom Newton has previously indicated he wrote a letter.

144 "Old Grub" would marry both Dunn sisters. He married Emilin Dunn in 1863. After her death in 1872 he married her sister Mary Ann.

write at present. *The weather is fine. It rains about every other day. We are encamped with in eight miles of Vicksburg now. We havent had any muss with the sesesh lately. We are out scouting around in the country the greater part of our time. Get plenty of fresh pork and beef and a barn fesant occasionly. We are a going out about twenty miles today to burn a grist mill that the Rebs makes a practice of grinding on. We dont get mutch news lately of any importance from other parts of the army. Lieut Lucas has got back to the Company again. The health of the Regiment is better than it ever was before. Their isnt any sick man in the Regimental Hospital at the present time at all and the Doctor said he only had two calls for medicine yesterday. The next that will come to Illinois on furlows will be Wm Hall, Uriah Snider and Newt Canfield[145] of Chandlerville. The married men are all to get furlows first so you see that their will be no show for me to get a furlow this winter so you neednt look for me. You can eat your own turkey at Christmas and I will try to content myself with some of the southern poltry. I will send Mary a peace of a sesesh Valentine in this letter that I got from a sesesh girl a few days ago. Well I dont see any more sign of this war a comeing to a close than I did a six months ago but I hope it will wind up some time this winter for I havent mutch anxiety to stay down here an other summer cheating me out of lots of fun. I beleive I have written all that I can think of, so no more at present.*

Write soon. Yours with respect, AN Paschal.

---

145 Thomas Newton Canfield (114th Ill., Co. A) enlisted as private on August 14, 1862, was promoted to Sergeant, 1st Sergeant and Captain. He was mustered out on August 3, 1865.

Warren County, Mississippi, November 6, 1863

*Dear Sister [Mary]: It is with pleasure I take my pen to answer
your kind letter of the date of Oct the 17. I was very glad to hear
that you were well but feel sorry that Mothers health is so poor
this fall. I am well and hearty as usual and hope this will find
you the same. I havent anything of mutch importance to write
at present. Their hasnt been any thing going on in this part of
Dixie lately worth note. We received orders this morning to
pack up our duds and be ready to march tomorow morning at
six o'clock. We are first going to the City of Vicksburg and take
shipping either down the river or up but it is the impression of
all that we are going up to Memphis, Tenn[146] and I am of the
same opinion. Capt Johnson started home on a furlow three or
four days ago. It is the calculation to let the married men all
have furlows first, and as I do not represent one of that kind I
will have to wait a rite smart while yet for a furlow so you need
not look for me home this winter unless their should be such
good luck as the war to end. I would like to see you all first rate,
but I belong to Old Uncle Sam and he dont let his boys roam
everywhere they please thats so. Lieut Lucas has returned to the
Company and is now in command of the famous Co A of the
114 Regt Ills Vol. I read in a Memphis paper today that Abe had
made a call for three thousand more men to help put down this
rebellion and if they cant be got by volunteering their will be
apt to be a draft and then they will have to come willing or not.
I hope the Union feeling is still kept up in the northern states
and I hope it will grow stronger every day and the traitors of
the north quiet down since the defeat of Vallandingham[147], and*

---

146 "About the 20th of November, left, on transports, for Memphis, and, on the 26th
of November, went on provost duty there." Adjutant General's Report.

147 Clement Vallandigham was an Ohio Congressman, the son of a preacher married
to a Maryland planter's daughter. He campaigned for the Democratic nomination
for Governor of Ohio on a peace platform, calling upon soldiers to desert, declar-
ing the South invincible, etc. He was arrested and tried for treason, but Lincoln
commuted his sentence to banishment in the South. He was nominated for Governor, but lost the election.

others believe that. I will stop writing for this time. Write soon,
so no more at present.

Yours with respect, A.N. Paschal

On November 8, 1863, the men of the 114th Illinois boarded boats in Vicksburg and headed north to Memphis, arriving there on November 12th. It had been eight months since they left Memphis to participate in the siege of Vicksburg.

By most accounts they were glad to be back, though Newton does complain about the cooler weather. They were put on provost duty. In other words, they became military policemen in the occupied city. This would certainly offer Newton an opportunity to practice his favorite pastime: Getting acquainted with southern girls.

It is impossible to say whether or not Newton visited prostitutes, but prostitution was rampant in Memphis during the occupation. Beale Street, now so famous for its music, was the center of this trade with numerous houses of prostitution. So many soldiers contracted venereal diseases that the U.S. army eventually legalized "the world's oldest profession" in Memphis and in Knoxville, Tennessee by employing doctors to monitor its safety. The Journal's "Observer" wrote from Memphis on December 26, 1863, that, "…some little irregularities may be expected among some of the officers and men in the various commands of this city of temptations."

Newton laments the fact that he is low on the list for a furlough, which usually went to married men first. Stuck in Memphis doing his duty, Newton would miss important family events transpiring some 400 miles away in Beardstown. He missed the death and funeral of his mother, Sally Street Paschal, and the marriage of his brother William. Perhaps the long separation from loved ones contributed to Newton's sincere demonstration of sympathy for the refugees that flocked into Memphis from the Corinth, Mississippi area which, despite a Union victory in the spring of 1862, remained a hotbed of guerilla attacks and cavalry skirmishes.

The following eight letters were written during Newton's three months of provost duty in Memphis.

Memphis, Tennessee, November 18, 1863

Dear Brother: It is with pleasure I take my pen to answer yours of Oct the 26. I was very glad to hear from you all. I am well at present and hope this will find you all the same. Stuckey just arrived this evening. He was arrested at Camp Butler and had company all the way down. We landed here at Memphis on the twelfth. We are a doing provost guard duty now in the city and I expect that very likely we will stay here this winter. Our Company turned over the horses day before yesterday and now we do our traviling on foot. The weather is fine at present. You spoke of Fish offering that eighty of land that he bought of H. Garins and you think it can be bought for one thousand or less with reasonable payments. For my part I think that would be tollerable resonable. But it is hardly worth my while to say any thing about buying land while I am in the army only getting thirteen dollars per month. But I would like to have an interest in the farm pretty well. But you bet it is particular business to save any money in the army. But if you want to bye the land I will go in and help you all I can. I think that I can make enough to pay the interest and if you can get along with the principal. If this war should ever end I might help you with that for I had rather put money in land than in the Bank so I will leve it to you for you know more how times and things are in Illinois than I do. But if you bye I will go in and help you all I can if it is but little, and if you intend to rent land this comeing season you had better bye and save the trouble of renting. I have no news worth mentioning. Only we are a conscripting the citizens down here in Tennesee in to the Union Army. Their was twenty five put in an Indiana Reg today. So no more tonight. Yours with respect, A. N. Paschal PS. Write soon and give me the news.

Memphis, Tennessee, November 20, 1863

Dear Brother [Will]: It is with pleasure I take my seat this morning to scratch you a few lines. I wrote you a letter day before yesterday but thought that I would write a again and let you know that I had sent twenty five dollars by express to Leonard & Co Bank, Beardstown, to you. I expressed the money yesterday so I think it will get there about as soon as this letter if not sooner. I would have had more to of sent if I hadnt of drew quite so many clothes. We are allowd 42 dollars a year for clothes and all we draw over that amount is taken out of our pay. Some of the boys drew as high as 60 dollars worth last year but we will be allowd fifty dollars for clothing this season but clothing is higher and I expect it will amount to the same after all. I have no news of any importance to write. The weather is very cold, windy and a raining to day and has the appeerence of snow soon. You bet the boys grumbles enough about leveing Vicksburg and comeing north as far as Memphis to stay this winter after being down there all summer. I saw Henry Gants[148] yesterday. He stays in Memphis. You spoke of buying that land of Fishes. If you do you may use all the money of mine towards paying for it. You may keep that horse of mine and work him if you need him but if you do not need him you may sell him but if you need him on the farm you had better keep him. I havent had a letter from Old Sarrel for some time but I reckon he is about there yet. I got a letter from Sister Margaret & Alec the other day. This was written in a hurry. I do not know weather you can read it or not. I have to go on guard in about ten minutes, so no more at present. Yours with respect, A. N. Paschal PS write soon.

---

148 Henry Gans (*Gans)

Memphis, Tennessee, December 5, 1863

Dear Sister: It is with pleasure I take my pen to answer your welcom letter of Nov the 27. I was glad to hear from you and that you were well but feel very sorry that Mothers is still troubled with the chills and fever. I am well and hope this will find you all enjoying good health. I havent any news of any importance to write at present. We are still at Memphis but their is a little talk of our leveing here and taking to the field for amusment, but for my part I had a little rather stay in town this winter. But if we are needed worse any where else I am willing to go for I think the 114 is able to stand its hand anywhere that any other Regt can that is in the supervise of Uncle Sam. I suppose you have heard of the hard battle and victory won by the western troops about Chattanooga[149] but still the war continues and but little signs as yet of its comeing to a close. I have give up all hope of its comeing to a close this winter and I would not be surprised if next winter was decked with tented fields in those southern states, for the sesesh appear as determined as they ever did and it will cost us considerable time yet to reduce and take possession of all of their strong positions still in their grasp. If they would give up when are whipped it would be quite different but they still openly declare that they will dye in the last ditch before they will come under a goverment with Abraham Lincoln at its head. Many are making their words good for a great many has breathed their last in the last six months in ditches. Our Reg is in excellent health this winter. Henry Freeman and James Berry are both well but Darwin Linsley has had another hard spell of sickness. He is getting a little better. He is in

---

149 The major battle for Chattanooga began on November 23. After battles for Lookout Mountain and Missionary Ridge, the Confederate forces retreated across Chickamauga Creek during the night of November 25, leaving Chattanooga and the surrounding area in control of Union forces.

the hospital. Taylor Pedigo[150] and wife are in Memphis but I havent went to see them yet. You spoke of Cousin Joe Street but I havent heard from him since you wrote to me about him. I have made inquiries in Co 3rd Ills Cav but cant get any clew of Thos Cuppys whereabouts but it is the general suposition of all that he is dead. Not even his officers know any of him. I would like to be up in Illinois this Christmas but they have quit granting furlows for a while. Charles Lawson[151] started home on what is called a sick furlow. A horse fell down with him and hurt his limb, as Isabelle[152] terms it improper to speak otherwise, and disabled him from duty for a spell. I got a letter from Alfie Brown yesterday. He said that John Horn[153] and family and all the rest of our connection were selling out there in that country[154]. So no more this time. Write again soon and give me the news. A. N. Paschal PS. Tell Will that I sent twenty five dollars by express. Wrote to him about the same time but he might have not got the letter.

Memphis, Tennessee, December 16, 1863

Dear Brother [Joe]: I now take my pen to answer your kind letter of Dec the 1st. I was very glad to hear from you all and that you were well but was very sorry to learn that mother still had the ague and could not get any thing to break it up. I think that the doctors are but little acount or they could cure it. My health is good and has been ever since last spring. But we have lost another one of our Co by the name of Robert

---

150 William Taylor Pedigo (114th Illinois, Co. D). He mustered out on June 1, 1865(*Pedigo)

151 Charles Lawson (114th Ill., Co. A) was mustered out August 3, 1865. (*Lawson)

152 Isabelle Paschal (1844-1924) was Newton's cousin, the daughter of Green Hill and Sarah (Deweber) Paschal. She married James W. Hiles on March 21, 1872, in Cass County, Illinois. She is buried in the Walnut Grove Cemetery, Virginia, Illinois.

153 John Horn was Newton's cousin, son of his deceased aunt, Emily Paschal Horn.

154 Nemaha County, Nebraska.

McCarty[155]. He died in the hospital on the night of the 14th inst with the intermitent fever. I expect you knew him. He was a miller by trade and ust to work at Fishes mill. The weather is very wet and cold down here at present. It has been raining for a week and is still raining. It will soon be Christmas down here and we expect to have a pretty good time here in Memphis. Last Christmas we marched all day. I wish that I could be at home and spend Christmas but their is no show to get there so I will try to content my self with a Dixie Christmas this time. I havent any news concerning the war to write worth mentioning at present only we are getting quite a number of conscripts in Memphis. I would like very well to be out hunting and trapping this winter. I think that I could make money faster than I do in souldiering at thirteen doll ars a month for I see fur is a very good price this winter and likely to be higher in the spring. I would like to see this war wind up this winter but their aint any more sign of this war a closing than their was this time last year. I dont make any other calculations getting out of the army until I have surved my three years out. My time will soon be half out. I have surved sixteen months of my time already and I am getting along fine. We are living in our tents yet but we are a building barracks and will have them done in about three days and then we will move into them. I think we will get along fine this winter if we are not called to go some place else. But their is one thing in Memphis that I dont like very well and that is the small pox. Some of the boys in Co D has got them now but their hasnt been deathes with that disease yet in our Regt. I got a letter from old Grub the same time I got yours and I will answer it in a few days. I would answer it today but I am hoping to put up chimneys to the barracks and havent time.

So no more at present, write soon. Yours with respect, A. N. Paschal

---

155 Robert McCarty (114th Ill, Co. A). The Adjutant General's Report states he died at Memphis, Tennessee on December 16, 1863. (*McCarty)

Memphis, Tennessee, December 18, 1863

Dear Brother [Will]: It is with pleasure I take my pen to answer your kind letter of Dec the 1st. I was very glad to hear from you and that you were well but am very sorry that Mothers health is so poor this winter. My health is good and I hope those few lines will find you all enjoying the same. We moved into our new barracks to day and we are pretty well fixt for winter. Our Regt is divided off by Companies in different parts and each Co has its own streets to guard and so we know one day what we will have to do the next and that is some satisfaction for we can have our meals regular. I still have a negro wench to cook and do my washing but still I had rather eat some white womans cooking, but I had rather eat a darkeys than to do the cooking myself. I pay one dollar per month for my cooking and washing. I havent any thing of any importance to write at present only it appears that it takes my letters considerable time to get through to Illinois of late but perhaps they are a little like myself, to lazy to travel fast. I sent you a note in answer to that one you sent me by Mr. Stuckey the next day after I recieved and told you that I was willing to go in with you and buy that peace of land owned by Mr. Fish but I presume you have got my note before this time. If you never got it this will show that I am willing that you should purchase it and that I am willing to help you all I can on the payment of the same and then afterwards divide it or dispose of it to one another just as we see fit or agreed upon for I had rather own land in Illinois than to keep greenbacks on hand. You spoke of a couple of weddings and the likely hood of more betwixt them and Christmas & you did not know but what Old Grub would get in the notion to follow suit. And I will say go on Old Grub, never renig as long as you have a trump to play for trick it is good at almost any stage of the game. I answered Blakes letter day before yesterday. I want you to tell the girls to not wait for the souldiers to come home but to get married the first good oppertunity and my advice to all of you civillians of the masculine gender is to pitch in and get you a frau before the war closes or else you might meet with some opposition that would not be very congenial to your feelings for it is the intention of almost all of the young souldiers to get married pretty soon after they are mustered out of the supervise of Uncle Sam. We had a little snow storm yesterday morning and it has been pretty mutch like winter to day. I will wind up this letter hoping to hear from you again soon. So no more at present. Yours with respect, A. N. Paschal

Memphis, Tennessee, December 24, 1863

Dear Sister [Mary]: It is with a sad heart I sit down this evening to answer your letter bearing date of Dec the 18th, stating the death of our beloved Mother[156] *but I had heard of the our loss before I received your letter. I do not suppose that any one could suffer her loss more than myself but thank God she was prepared for the solemn realities of death and I have no doubt but she is better off now. She must of suffered a great deal with her sickness for she had been very unwell all fall but I hadnt any idea that she was so low until I recieved Bro William's last letter witch said that she had a very bad cough and I knew that she was pretty bad off for she had had so many hard attacks of that before that she could not stand it long. I was very sorry to hear that you had been sick but I hope that you are better. I want you take good care of yourself until you get better. I am well at present and hope this will find you all the same. Their has been two died in our Reg lately with the small pox. Their is several others that has had it lately*

---

156 Sarah "Sally" Street Paschal was born in 1810 in Tennessee, the fifth of eight children born to Anthony and Elizabeth Street. On August 8, 1830, in Morgan County, Illinois, she married Coleman Paschal. Her husband preceded her in death in April of 1852. Sarah died on December 11, 1863, and is buried in Griggs Cemetery, Cass County.

but I believe that they are all getting well. We havent had any cases in our Co yet. I believe all of the boys in our company has been vax inated. I havent any news of any importance to write. I want you to write and let me know what you intend to do whether you still allow to stay there on the farm or break up house keeping. I hope William will attend to all of the business that will have to be attended to for I expect that he knows more how things is than any one else. I wish that I could of been at home and seen Mother before her death but I expect you know that their are but little chance for a souldier to go and see their friends. I tryed to get to come home last fall but I could not and their is no chance of my comeing home yet. Tomorrow is Christmas but it will be a sad one to me on account of our bereavements, Mother, sister & nease[157] are all gone but I hope that they are in heaven and are happy. I hope when we come to that day that we will be prepared to meet them there in that better land. We are still in Memphis. Our Company is enjoying good health and are in good spirits and the most of them think that this cruel war will end next summer. I wish that it might end sooner but I do not expect we will go in [missing piece of letter] field again next summer and [piece missing] will be with sucsess. You did not put your name to your letter but I knew it by the writing. I want you to write again soon. So no more tonight. Excuse bad writing for the boys are shaking the table pretty near all the time. From your brother, A. N. Paschal

Memphis, Tennessee, January 14, 1864

Dear Brother [Will]: I take my pen this evening to write you a few lines. I havent received any letters from you of late. I am well at present and hope this may find you and the rest

---

157 His mother Sarah Street Paschal, sister Harriet Paschal Skinner, and niece Grace.

*of the family well. The weather is very disagreable at present.
The ground is covered with ice and sleet and it is begining
to snow now. Their is nothing of any importance going on
in this section of the Country. Orderly Hitchcock[158] has been
promoted to a Lieutenancy in a Negro Regiment. Their is not
anything else happened to Co A worth note. We had a pretty
good time a Christmas and New Years. Their was plenty of
dances and plenty of pretty girls and the time passed off finely.
Grub, I am informed that you have been joined in the bonds
of wedlock with Miss Emma Dunn[159]. I feel a little slighted
not being invited to the wedding but I will pardon you for
not sending me an invite and wish you both mutch joy and
happiness. I hope you will make a good husband and her a
good wife. I heard of your marriage on the 2nd of this month.
I got the tidings in a letter sent to Jacob Stuckey by his father.
We allways get our latest news through that source. I hardly
know what to write for I am looking for a letter from you
daily but I can excuse you for not writing lately on account
of you having more important duty. I am left to dance in the
pig troft at last but that isnt a very hard job for me for I have
had considerable experience in dancing and understand the
business pretty well. I understand that their is to be a draft
in Illinois pretty soon and when it does come off I want you
to write to me and let me know whether it catches you or
not. James Blanford[160] has came back to the Reg but he has to
stand a court martial for being away so long and will be apt
to loose about seven months pay if not more. I heard yesterday*

---

158 Norman S. Hitchcock was promoted to 1st Lt, Co. K, 71st U. S. Colored Infantry on June 12, 1864. (*Hitchcock)

159 William Paschal married Emlin Dunn on December 24, 1863, and they had five children. Emlin died on September 8, 1872, and William married her sister, Mary Ann Dunn, on December 17, 1873, and they had two children. William died February 3, 1917, and is buried in Diamond Grove Cemetery in Jacksonville, Illinois.

160 James C. Blanford (114th Ill, Co. A) was 16 years old when he enlisted on August 5, 1862. He was mustered out on August 3, 1865. (*Blanford)

that your old preacher, Mr. Barwick[161], had been killed with a cannon ball striking him on the head and completely sepperating it from his body but I hope it is not true. I believe that I have written all that I can think of at present so I will stop writing at present. Hoping to hear from you soon. Give my best wishes to all inquiring friends and accept the same for yourself. Yours truly, A. N. Paschal PS. This ink is so poor I fear that you cant read this that I have written.

Memphis, Tennessee, January 26, 1864

Dear Sister [Mary]: It is with pleasure I sit down this evening to answer your kind letter which I received a few days ago. I was very glad to hear that you are well again and all of the rest of the relation. I wrote Will a letter this morning and I havent but little news to write. I am well and hope this will find you all enjoying good health. I expect that we will leve this place in a few days. We will go down the river when we start. I think that we will go down as far south as Mobile. I dont mutch like the idea of going south again this spring. If they had of left us down there all winter I would not of cared so mutch for we would of been more used to the climate. I have just been out to see the poor famlies that has moved in from around Corinth. They are almost destitute of everything. I have seen lots of people in a pretty destitute condition but I think these famlies are in the worst fix that any I have seen yet. I wish that this war would soon end but I havent any idea that it will any ways soon. George Rhinebarger has reinlisted and passed by here on his way home. He has leave to stay in the state of Illinois

---

161 Rev. Joseph Sidney Barwick, chaplain for the 85th Illinois Regiment, was born in 1815 in Maryland. Fortunately, he did not get his head blown off by a cannon ball. He was mustered out at Camp Butler on June 11, 1865, and died in Shelby County, Missouri at the age of 75 in 1890. (*Barwick)

*thirty days. I was payed of the other day and sent twenty
dollars by him. I put it in an envelope and directed it to Will.
I would like to be in Illinois this spring to go to work and
raising corn. I think that it would suit me fully as well as
souldiering. But I am just like an Old German was in our Co
when we started from Camp Butler. He said he was sworn in
and had to be gone. I hope you and Tommy will get a long
well but I know you must feel very lonesome without our
dear mother to keep you company. But I hope you are in a
situation to take a good care of yourselves. I expect that Tom
is quite a lad by this time. I got a letter from sister Rachel the
other day she said that they were all well. It is getting late
so I will stop writing. Write soon and give me the news. No
more at present. Your brother, A.N. Paschal*

On the same day that Newton wrote the above letter, his cousin Lt. Henry Freeman also penned a letter to Mary. It is one of two letters from Freeman that Mary preserved. The other, which appears later in this book, reveals Newton's capture by Confederate soldiers. This letter is of a less serious nature and is in response to a letter written by Mary. Freeman has excellent penmanship but as the reader will see his spelling left a bit to be desired. His choice of words to capitalize is also interesting. Freeman makes an awkward attempt to sound like a wise preacher as he tries to console his young cousin over the loss of her mother. And he clearly shows his displeasure at the possibility that his cousin Will (Old Grub) has stolen his Miss Dunn. It is unknown which of the two sisters that Freeman fancied but Will Paschal would eventually marry both of them. Freeman married Sophia Bassett in 1866 and one of their daughters, Grace Eliza, would live until 1971, dying at the age of 100.

Memphis, Jan. 26, 1864

My Dear Friend Mary Paschal,

Yours of Jan. 13 was received with Pleasure a few days ago. As you Hoped it found me Enjoying good helth, for whitch we should always feel grateful.

I was glad to hear of your good helth and that life as it is with you in its spring-time is passing so pleasantly and hapy and although the bereavement you spoke of the loss of a Mother seams hard to be born, and in our weakness would fain call Her back to Earth. Yet the Christian feels thankful for the asurence that they are so Mutch Better off and feel too that one Spirit is Wating and watching to welcome one to glory.

One tie more loosed from Earth and bound to Heaven. One more Angel whose spirit hovers round our pathway and seems to say be faithful that you may enjoy the bliss that is in resurrection for the richous. We can but say with Daniel of Old Thy canot return to us but we will go to them.

I saw Newt a few days ago. He is in good helth and seams pretty well satisfied. We are having butiful wether now. Here it seems almost like May. The Citizins think we will have some Hard wether yet. The prospects are at present that we wile move from this place Soon. Most Probily down the River again but it is not certain.

Memphis is a pretty live place but it is was not for Peopel from the North and West here I think morals would be at rather a low end. I think at least ½ of the population of the place are Catholicks. Yet the Catholicks are not the worst people in the world.

We hav good advantages hear for religious servis. Church and Sabath scool on Sunday and Prais meetings during the week.

For these reasons and advantages I would like to remain hear for a while at least.

Since Will is married I am glad he has got an agreeable companion for that seams to me is the greate secret of Lifes Hapiness or Misery. You don't know whether he married my Miss Dunn or not. Well I don't know that I do Eather but he does and if he has taken advantage of my absents and done that thing well I wont Promise what I'll do. But I do think it was real mean if he did it, don't you?

If we go down the river and we are again to undergo the hardships of land on dreary Marches it will be (more than Ever if Possabel) a pleasure to secure letters from My Friends at Home and tharabouts. I hope you will not forget to write to me again soon.

Your Friend, H.D. Freeman

On February 5, 1864, the 114th Illinois, under the command of General Stephen A. Hurlbut, left Memphis on a scouting mission. They were ordered to help clear the way for the Union cavalry led by General William Sooy Smith. Smith and his men were expected to rendezvous with General William T. Sherman in Meridian, Mississippi. The men of the 114th did their job and fought off a rebel force they encountered at Wyatt, Mississippi. But as with the Battle of Jackson, Newton missed out on the action. He explained that he "went out with the Reg 45 miles and there they sent a part of the wagons to Memphis and I went with them to help guide them back."

With the road from Memphis now clear General Smith embarked with a cavalry force of 7,000. They were slowed by the weather and perhaps by Sooy Smith's overly cautious advance. They were also harassed and kept at bay by the smaller cavalry force of Nathan Bedford Forrest in skirmishes at West Point and Okolona, Mississippi. Meanwhile, on February 14th, Sherman roared into Meridian from the west, obliterating rail lines, depots, arsenals and even hospitals – anything that might be of aid to the Confederacy.

The Confederate force, under the command of General Leonidas Polk, the cousin of the late President James K. Polk, could not stop Sherman from occupying Meridian. However, Sherman needed Smith's cavalry force to continue. After six days waiting in Meridian, Sherman finally gave up on Sooy Smith and returned to Vicksburg. At that point Forrest went after Smith and quickly chased him back to Memphis in what became known sarcastically as "The Sooy Smith Expedition."

Newton seemed content to be back on provost duty, although the 114th was eventually pulled out of the city and moved to a camp a few miles east of Memphis. In one of his more amusing letters Newton writes to his little brother Tommy (Blake) on February 21, 1864, and tells him, "There is lots of girls here in Memphis and you bet I have lots of fun for you know that I am quite a ladys man and pretty good looking to boot."

Newton wonders if the 114th might spend the entire summer in Memphis. He also hopes for a summer furlough to return to Beardstown and see the family that he has not seen in nearly two years. But the summer of 1864 had a much different fate in store for Pvt. Asa Newton Paschal.

Memphis, Tennessee, February 19, 1864

Dear Brother [Will]: It is with pleasure I sit down to answer your kind letter of Feb the seventh. I was glad to hear from you and that you were all well I am well and hope this may find you all the same. I have been away from Memphis for a few days. Our Brigade has been out upon a scout as far as the Tallahatchie River[162]. I wasnt with the Reg all of the time but I done about as mutch marching as if I had been along all of the time. I went out with the Reg 45 miles and there they

---

162 "On February 5, 1864, Regiment left on a scout, and engaged the enemy at Wyatt, Miss.--enabling the cavalry, under General W. S. Smith, to cross the Tallahatchie above, at New Albany. Then returned to Memphis, and went again on provost duty." Adjutant General's Report

*sent a part of the wagons to Memphis and I went with them
to help guide them back. We stayed in Memphis two days and
then we laid in a fresh lot of grub and started out and met the
Brigade. We got back yesterday. We are now in our barracks
again and doing patrole duty again and I would not wonder if
we stayed here all summer. The Brigade had but little trouble
with the sesesh while it was out. We took three prisnors and
lost none. The weather has been very cool for the last three
or four days. The boys are in pretty good health at this time
but the small pox still visits our camp occasionly. We have
got one case of it in our company. He took it while he was out
upon the march. He has been sent to the hospital. His name
is Leonard Walter[163]. He is a Dutchman. Their is no news of
any importance in town at present. I have got this letter mixt
up and did not tell you the object of our scouts. We was sent
out to the Tallahatchie River to draw the attention of the Rebs
at one place. The cavalry sucseeded in crossing at an other
place. The Cavalry all got across safe and are now going down
through Mississippi and I do not expect that they will stop
this side of Mobile. Their is between thirty and forty thousand
of the cavalry gone on the raid. I havent heard but little of
Shermans[164] expadition yet but I dont expect that he is idle.
Tell Tommy that I will answer his this evening but I have to go
on guard and I havent time. Give my love to all. Write soon,
so no more this time. Yours truly, A. N. Paschal*

Memphis, Tennessee, February 21, 1864

*Dear Brother [Tommy]: It is with pleasure I take my pen
this morning to answer your kind letter of Feb the 7th. I was
very glad to hear from you and that you are well. I am well*

---

163 Leonard Walter (114th Ill, Co. A) died at Memphis, Tennessee on March 3, 1864.

164 Maj. Gen. William Tecumseh Sherman (1820-1891) was commanding the Army
and the Department of the Tennessee when this letter was written.

and hope this will find you all the same. I dont know that I
have any thing to write that would amuse you at present. I
wrote Grub a letter day before yesterday and gave him all
of the news that I could think of. Tennessee are rather dull
about here since the troops left and went down the River. I
got a letter from Lime Hager[165] the other day and he said
that the Sangamon River was a rising very fast at that time.
But I hope it will not get high enough to do any damage. You
say that you intend to farm with Old Grub this summer. I
dont want you to work to hard. I hope that you may have a
fine time a farming and do well for I do not expect to come
and help you farm this season and perhaps I may not next
but I hope I may. My time is half out a working for Uncle
Sam. Blake, their is lots of girls here in Memphis and you
bet I have lots of fun for you know that I am quite a ladys
man and pretty good looking to boot. Tommy, I would like
to know whether you are a getting along with the girls or
whether you lead them around mutch or not for I expect that
you are quite a lad by this time. I would like to see you all
very well but I havent any show that I will get a furlow this
summer for they are pretty hard to get hold of lately unless
a fellow would reinlist and I never will take one upon them
terms you bet. The weather is very nice and quite spring like
and I hope that the weather is nice up there. We had meeting
in our barracks to day at ten oclock and we have meeting
once a week regular. I believe that I have written enough for
this time. Write soon and give me the news, so no more this
time. Yours, A. N. Paschal

---

165 The Lyman Hager family was a near neighbor of the Coleman Paschal family.
(*Hager)

Memphis, Tennessee, February 28, 1864

Dear Sister [Mary]: It is with pleasure I seat myself this evening to answer your kind letter which I was very thankful to receive for I was very ancious to hear from sister Margaret. I was very glad to learn that she was getting better and that the rest of the folks were well. This leves me in the enjoyment of good health. I beleve their is but one sick that belongs to our Co. His name is Leonard Walter. He is in the hospital. His disease is the small pox but he is getting along fine and if he has no backset he will soon be well again. I have written to Will & Tommy lately so I will not write in this letter what we have been doing since I last wrote to you but I will give you the latest news that is in town. The Cavalry force that left here some time about the first of the month that we thought were going to go south and join Gen Sherman has returned. They were only sent out to draw the attention of the Rebs while Sherman could accomplish his move below. The Cavalry done considarble loss both in killed and prisnors. The loss of the enemy fully as great. I havent any late news from Shermans army but at the last account he was moving strait foward. I have saw several of the boys since they got back. I have seen Morris Schaffer[166], Wm Nicholson[167], Martin Treadway[168] and others that I am acquainted with. The weather has been very nice down here in Dixie for some time but it is cloudy misting rain to day. It has been quite spring like. The peach trees are in full bloom and the gardens and flowers and srubery looks very nice but I am of the opinion that you cant [like it] as mutch as Ills at the present time. We are still doing duty in town and living in our barracks. I havent any idea how long we will stay here. We may leave pretty soon and we may stay all summer. Our Brigade

---

166 John Morris Schaeffer (*Schaeffer)

167 William Nicholson (Third Cavalry, Co. C) enlisted on August 19, 1861, and mustered out September 5, 1864. (*Nicholson)

168 Martin Treadway (Third Cavalry, Co. F) enlisted on May 26, 1861. (*Treadway)

Commander has command of the post. James Blanford from down about Indian Creek that was home so long has been courtmartialed and sent inside of the fort to work thirty days at hard labor and all of his pay stopped from the time that he left the hospital at St. Louis. I would like very well to be up home this spring but their is no sign of my getting up there this spring or summer. I may get a furlough this summer but it is very doutful but their is one thing certain my time is half out and I shant reinlist on any terms. It is getting late and I shall stop writing for this time. Answer soon, give my love to all inquiring friends. Your Brother, A. N. Paschal

Memphis, Tennessee, March 9, [1864][169]

Dear Brother [Joe]: It is with pleasure I sit down this morning to answer your kind letter of Feb the 26th. I was very glad to hear from you and that you were well but I was sorry that your wife was unwell but I hope she is better. My health is good and I hope this may find you all enjoying a reasonable portion of [good] health. I havent any news worth mentioning at the present time. We are still in the city and getting along finely. Mr. Rienberger arived here last evening on his way to his regiment. The weather is very nice and spring like and has appearence of rain this morning. You said if I had any claims against the estate[170] except notes that I had better send in my bill for you had advertised for an adjustment of claims. I once had some accounts that was not settled up but I reckon that I have lost them all for I havent any of them with me so I will just let them go and say no more about them for I expect that things are tangled up enough any way. I once had a day book with several little items in it but I disremember what I

---

169 This letter, and the letter of Feb. 28th, were dated 1863, but the contents of both letters dictate that Newton should have written 1864.

170 The estate of his mother.

did with it. I may of gave it to Sister Mary or I may of lost it.
I hope that you may not have mutch trouble in settling up the
business. We had a wedding in Co A last Sabbath. The mans
name was Thomas Moore[171]. He was maried to a Miss Tuft.
They gave the Company a splended dinner and we had a good
time you bet. Tell Em that Haywood[172] is well and hearty and
the balance of the Company is doing well. I would like to be
in Illinois this spring to go to farming for I get so lazy a sould-
iering this nice weather that I cant rest. I think a little work
would be an advantage to me at present. I still keep a darkie to
do my cooking and washing. I have come to the conclusion that
it was never intended for me to do my own cooking. I wrote
Hutchinson a letter a day or two ago. The last letter that I got
from him they were all getting better but I suppose that Sister
Margaret had a pretty hard time with the fever, but I hope that
she will soon be up again. The boys are playing dominos on the
table and bothered me all of the time while I was writing this
but I hope that you can read it. Write soon and give me the
news. So no more at present. Yours A. N. Paschal

Much transpired that would have caught the interest and elicited comments from the opinionated Asa Newton Paschal during the months of
March, April and May, 1864, but no letters written between March 9th
and May 15th survived. It is likely that Newton wrote many letters during this time but they were not among those passed down by his sister
Mary. Perhaps his letters never reached her.

On March 9th, the very day that Newton wrote to his brother Joe,
President Abraham Lincoln promoted U.S. Grant to Lieutenant General, making Grant the commander of all Union armies. Grant quickly
convened meetings with General George Meade and his close friend
General William T. Sherman to devise a master plan to end the war.

---

171 Thomas Moore (114th Ill, Co. A) was mustered out as a corporal on July 30, 1865.
(*Moore)

172 Emeline Haywood Knight, sister of Joseph Haywood. (*Haywood)

Grant would focus on Robert E. Lee and his Army of Northern Virginia. Sherman would advance through Georgia on his legendary Atlanta Campaign, the success of which would make Sherman one of the most important military figures in world history.

Confederate General Joseph Johnston, the man so hesitant to rescue Vicksburg, was in charge of stopping Sherman from sacking Atlanta. The cavalry genius Nathan Bedford Forrest would attempt to disrupt the increasingly important Union supply lines from the Mississippi. Forrest successfully attacked Union City, Tennessee and Paducah, Kentucky on March 24th and 25th. Then on April 12th the usually calculated Forrest allowed his emotions and racism to get the better of him in the infamous Ft. Pillow Massacre. After compelling the Union fort on the banks of the Mississippi River to surrender, Forrest apparently allowed his soldiers to butcher the black soldiers that comprised half of the fort's Union force of 557 men. The rebel cavalry used their bayonets to slaughter the unarmed men.

The Illinois 114th was a mere 45 miles to the south in Memphis, but they were not summoned to help defend the fort.

The reaction to the Ft. Pillow Massacre was swift and detrimental to the hopes of the South. Northern resolve was strengthened and "colored" troops were honored for their service and sacrifice. Three days after the massacre the conservative yet pro-Union governor of Tennessee, Andrew Johnson, announced his support for emancipation. On April 17th Lt. Gen. Grant ordered that prisoner exchanges must include black prisoners held by the South. This effectively ended prisoner exchanges. But it did not slow Forrest who continued to disrupt supply lines destined for Sherman's huge force in Georgia. Also on April 17th Mary Paschal wrote a letter to her brother. It is the only known letter written to Newton that survived the war and it is printed below.

In late May General Sherman ordered a large contingent of Union cavalry and infantry to leave Memphis and engage Forrest, who was reported to be gathering his forces near Tupelo, Mississippi. Unfortunately for Newton and the men of the Illinois 114th, Sherman trusted the wrong man to lead this critical assault. His name was General Samuel Sturgis. The engagement would be known as the Battle of Brice's Cross Roads. It would virtually destroy the 114th and it would end the communications from Newton to his family back in Beardstown. But before he departed on this fateful campaign he wrote two more letters home. No other letters by Newton Paschal have survived and it is likely that after the Battle of Brice's Cross Roads he was never heard from again. The summer furlough he hoped for would be a summer of hell, in Andersonville.

Letter to Newton
From His Sister, Mary Paschal

Chapin, Illinois, April 17, 1864

Dear Brother:

With pleasure I sit down to write to you. It has been some time since I have heard from you. The last letter Will received. In the first place I will tell you I am at Sister Margarets this evening enjoying good health. Sister is better, but is not able to do any work yet. She washes the dishes sometimes and that is all of the housework. The rest of the family is well. I left home two weeks ago yesterday. They were all well then. I have not heard directly from there since.

I am teaching school at the Green Meadow School House near here, which commenced the 11th of April. I got along very well last week and hope to continue in so doing. I am to get $20 a month. I went home and stayed some over two weeks. Time flew rapidly and I had a pleasant time, but home is not like it was when my own dear mother was there, far from it. I hated to come up here so far away from home on Tommy's account. He will miss me most. Will has another to keep him company so that he does not miss me so much. My leaving home to teach this time was so far different from what it was before, I could not help but think of it. Mother went out of the house with me and you leaned on the gate post and told *me not to cry. Now, no mother, and you so far away. Rachel and the children were well when I came away. Thaniel was complaining of a sore knee, which hurt him considerable. I received a letter from Cousin Joseph Street. He has got home. He did not say whether he had been discharged or not but I suppose he has. The relation were all tolerable well except Uncle Bland[173]. He was very sick. The relation in this part of the state are all well as far as I know. Josh Crow was up to Beardstown this spring on a visit with his wife and child. I did not see them as I was up here when they were here, also James Crow has been back, but I did not see him either. This is Sunday evening. I have stayed in the house almost all day. This is rather a lonesome place on Sunday, there being no meeting or Sunday School here and the cars not running makes it more so. I can see soldiers on the cars every day, but the one I would rather see than any other is yourself. I would like to know if you have ever heard from Mr. Richards again. I once heard he was in prison at Richmond but I have never heard anything since.*

Please direct to Chapin, Morgan Co., Ills, when you write. Tell me all the news in general. It is getting late and I must quit for tonight. Now may our heavenly Father protect you and give you health and bring you home safe is the prayer of your Sister Mary E. Paschal.

P. S., Please write soon. Good by for this time. Margaret & the children sends their love to you, except [accept] the same from your Sister Mary.

---

173 James Bland was married to Mary Street, oldest sister of Sarah (Street) Paschal. They lived in Lee County, Iowa.

Memphis, Tennessee, May 15, 1864

Dear Brother: With mutch pleasure I take my pen to answer your letter of April the 16th. It has been some time since I received your letter but I havent had time until now to answer it. I had just started out upon a march when received it but now I am back at Memphis. I am well and hope this may find you all the same. I havent anything of any importance to write at present. We have moved out of town about a mile and are doing picket duty. I was very glad to get out of town this spring for I think it will be healthier but I would like to be in town next winter again. The weather is tollerable warm down here for the time a year. We have plenty of shade trees in our camp to get under and not mutch to do only wallow around in the shade of them. We get a plenty to eat sutch as it is. It is sow belly, cottonwood bread, sugar & coffe, rice & beans and you bet that is a pretty strong diet for the spring of the year especily when we have to cook it ourselves. My old Negro cook took a fool notion and died a few days ago and I havent made a rase of another one yet. The health of the Reg is pretty good and I think that we are pretty lucky to be down here instead of being with the Potomac Army for I am of the opinion that it cant be very healthy where they use so many blue pills[174] as they do in that section of the Country. Their has been but little fighting around here for a long time. Gen Washburn[175], Commander of this Department, has issued an order to stop citizens from bying any thing in Memphis and takeing it out into the Country and has ordered the boats not to land at any place except millitary posts between Cairo and New Orleans. I suppose that it was done to stop the sesesh from living upon northern grub. If the news is correct about Grant's Army I

---

174 He may have been referring to a pill made with blue mass, a preparation containing powdered mercury, and used as a laxative.

175 Brig. Gen. Cadwallader C. Washburn (1818-1882), from Maine, was commanding District of West Tennessee, Army of the Tennessee, at the time of this letter.

think they will take Richmond this spring or do some pretty hard fighting for it but it always takes a month after a battle is fought to hear the strate of it and very often longer and very often never get the strate of it at all. Orange Sackett is back to the Co. I dont know yet whether I will get a furlough this summer or not. If I dont I reckon I will stay my time out and then take one for lifetime. I only have about a year and three months more to stay in the army any way. I believe that I have written enough for this time, write soon and send me the news.

Yours, A. N. Paschal

The Final Letter
of Asa Newton Paschal

Memphis, Tennessee, May 26, 1864

Dear Sister [Mary]: It is with pleasure I take my pen to write you a few lines in answer to your kind letter of April the 17th and hope you will pardon me for not writing sooner for I thought that I had answered your letter but this morning while I was looking over some old letters I found out my mistake. The way I came to neglect writing I had thirteen letters to answer at the same time and didnt have mutch time to write and had to answer them along as I had an oppertunity and by so doing I skipped yours and thought that I had them all answered. I havent any thing of any importance to write. I aint very well at present. I caught a cold a few days ago and it settled in my head. But I am getting better every day. It never stoped me from doing duty or drilling. We are doing pickett duty now and we have to drill four hours every day that we aint on guard. The weather is very warm and dry. The boys

*in general are pretty healthy although I will have to give the
name of one of our Co that departed life the 22nd inst. His
name was Jacob S. Stuckey. His disease was tyfoid fever. He
was sick about two weeks. He was taken sick while we was out
upon a scout after old Forrest[176]. I dont think that it is worth
while to say any thing about our scout for it didnt amount
to anything only marching the men around ten days for no
benefit at all. We get plenty of news here from other parts of
the army and hear of considerable fighting and according to
the papers our men are still gaining ground but not without
considerable loss. I still hope that this summers campaign
will wind up this war and give us peace once more. You spoke
about Mr. Richard of the Third Cavalry. I heard that he was
back to his Reg and now is in Memphis but I havent seen him
yet but I expect you have heard of his returning before now.
You say that you are teaching and get along well. I would like
to see you but furloughs has been stopped again and I doubt
whether their will be any more granted this summer so you
need not look for me to pay you a visit mutch before my time
is out. Our Co has been trying to get a transfer to the gun
boat servis but have not sucseeded in it yet. The boys are very
anxious to make a change in their servis but I expect that we
will still remain in the Infantry until our time expires. But if
we should get a transfer I will write and let you know. I believe
that I have written all that I can think of so no more this time.
Write soon. Give my love to all inquiring friends and receive
the same yourself. Your Brother, A.N. Paschal*

---

176 "On April 30, went on another scout, under General Sturgis, of a couple of weeks'
hard marching. Returned to Memphis, and was put on picket duty." Adjutant
General's Report.

Part Two

The Battle of Brice's Cross Roads

and the Capture of
Pvt. Asa Newton Paschal

General Nathan Bedford Forrest.

There is no record that Asa Newton Paschal wrote to his family in Beardstown after his letter of May 26, 1864. However, it is possible to track his movements over the first ten days of June, 1864. In late May the Illinois 114th received orders to head out with a large Union force under the command of Brigadier General Samuel Sturgis to track down the Confederate cavalry genius, General Nathan Bedford Forrest. The object was to stop Forrest from disrupting the supply lines of General Sherman's Union force.

At six in the morning on Wednesday, June 1, 1864, Newton boarded a train at the Memphis depot with his fellow members of the 114th Illinois and thousands of other Union soldiers. Also boarding the train, in separate cars, were Colonel Edwin Bouton's 55th and 59th US Colored Infantries. With the recent accusations of a massacre of black Union soldiers by Forrest and his Confederate troops at Fort Pillow, some white Union soldiers might have been nervous about encountering Forrest with the black troops at their side. Certainly many white soldiers, including Paschal, were racist in their attitudes toward blacks.

It shouldn't come as a surprise to the modern reader that the black troops proved to be among the most courageous in the Battle of Brice's Cross Roads, just as they were at every battle in which they participated. After all, African Americans had the most to lose if the South prevailed in the Civil War.

On that first night the troops bivouacked in Lafayette, Tennessee. Soldiers from the 114th witnessed Colonel William McMillen, the infantry commander, stagger and fall, presumably from drinking too much whiskey with General Sturgis aboard the train from Memphis. The following day, while the soldiers tried to stay dry during a torrential downpour, Sturgis and McMillen conferred over a bottle of whiskey. No movements were made.

On Friday morning, June 3rd the march was underway with Newton and Company A of the 114th in the lead. It was hot, muggy and pouring rain. Streams were swollen and supply wagons struggled to make progress in the deep mud. That night the troops set up camp in Lamar, Mississippi. On June 4th they made it as far as the Robinson farm, four miles east of Salem, Mississippi. June 5th was hot and dry. Sturgis and McMillan managed to advance the troops another six miles. As it turned out the officers should have taken better advantage of this brief break in the weather.

The Union forces set out again at 4 AM on Monday, June 6th and the weather took a turn for the worse. Heavy rain and lightening were not the only plagues endangering the weary troops. Rebel guerrillas were taking shots at the passing soldiers. They made it to Ripley, Mississippi by nightfall without any signs of Forrest.

That night some of the Union boys slipped out of camp to "forage". Such excursions usually netted fruit or vegetables with an occasional fowl or pig. But the industrious boys of the 114th returned with nine beef cattle. General Sturgis, staying in a private home and feasting on good food and drink, heard of the heist and ordered the soldiers to return the cattle to the rightful owner. This could not have been cheerfully obeyed since the troops were presently on half-rations of hardtack and one-fourth rations of meat.

While in Ripley rebel sympathizers spread rumors among the Union troops that Forrest was nearby with a force of 28,000. Widely believed to be true, it turned out to be a gross exaggeration. Forrest actually had about 5,000 soldiers with him. This may not have been a concern had the scouts that Newton refers to in his final letter been more successful. On June 7th the Union troops marched about five miles east of Ripley along Fulton Road and camped at another plantation. Once again the march was slowed by mud, but also by confusion on the part of the officers as to where the monstrous Confederate force was hiding.

The next two days of marching proved to be laboriously slow. The infantry caught up with the lead cavalry stuck in mud and quicksand. As their dark woolen uniforms became saturated with sweat, the weary soldiers drudged on through insufferable humidity. Fatigue from the strain of lifting heavy legs out of sucking mud caused many men to fall back. Some men collapsed from heat exhaustion. They finally settled for the night at the Stubbs Plantation about 14 miles southeast of Ripley.

Newton and his fellow troops arose at 5:30 AM on the fateful day of June 10, 1864. They noticed Sturgis and McMillan conferring over a bottle of whiskey before breakfast. Unfortunately, the officers would need full control of their faculties that day. The 114th was inspected at 7:30 AM. The men were ready to march but the road conditions would not allow it. The muddy roads would have to be corduroyed so that supply wagons could follow the troops. The day was already hot and muggy when they set out.

Men went through their canteens too quickly and were forced to replenish them with the lukewarm, gritty water from the Hatchie Bottom. Several miles ahead near Brice's Cross Roads the lead cavalry had finally stumbled into the Confederate forces of Nathan Bedford Forrest. They retreated and took cover. Word was sent back to Sturgis that the cavalry was greatly outnumbered by Confederate troops. This was not true. Nevertheless, Sturgis ordered McMilllan to "advance brigade up in quick time." The infantry troops were still about four miles from Brice's Cross Roads and the southern sun beat down unmercifully on their heavy, woolen uniforms. McMillan ordered them to run.

Perspiration poured out of men who had consumed their water properly. Saturated uniforms clung uncomfortably to their bodies. Other men did not sweat at all. Some collapsed from heat exhaustion or sunstroke. After two miles of running the men were allowed a short rest and then they resumed their run toward the rumble of artillery.

Sturgis had already arrived at Brice's Cross Roads on his horse. Certainly he was alarmed with what he saw. Rebel forces were spread out in every direction. They were battering the Union cavalry with canon balls and rifle fire. Sturgis frantically sent word to McMillan to quicken the pace. McMillan enforced the order and so when the troops finally arrived at Brice's Cross Roads they were literally staggering with fatigue and could scarcely hold their own rifles. Nevertheless, the

114th Illinois was ordered to relieve General Edwin Winslow's cavalry on Fulton Road. McMillan led the men into position ordering them to "hold the position at all hazards". Despite the immense fatigue from a four-mile run under a blazing sun these remarkable soldiers proved up to the challenge.

Forrest meant to take advantage of the weary Union troops and skirmishes began immediately. The 114th Illinois fought beside the 93rd Indiana. While rebel troops made progress elsewhere on the battlefields, the boys from Illinois and Indiana valiantly held their ground with minor loses. Fighting ceased temporarily at 1:30 PM. Forrest was using his time to prepare for, among other things, an all-out assault on the 114th and 93rd. When shooting erupted in nearby bushes Col. John King of the 114th told his men it was friendly fire. Indeed, the men of the 114th could see some blue uniforms in the bushes. But they remained suspicious and some wanted to fire back. Col. King ordered them not to, but a few fired anyway. They were right to do so; rebels were in the bushes.

By 1864 the C.S.A. war fund was so strapped that it was deemed logical to spend the diminishing resources on weapons rather than uniforms. Consequently, rebel soldiers often took to wearing just about any uniform they could get their hands on. Some of them even wore old Union uniforms, stolen or traded for from prisoners-of-war or simply taken off corpses after battles. Hence the confusion for the 114th as blue clad rebels from the 16th Tennessee came roaring out of the bushes with their blood curdling rebel yells.

The ensuing battle was savage. Much of it was hand to hand combat. The 93rd Indiana was forced to retreat under heavy rebel fire, exposing the right flank of the 114th. The rebel troops sought to take advantage and opened a fierce assault on the men of the 114th. The men from Illinois were not to be taken. Eventually the 16th Tennessee fell back to regroup with the 19th Tennessee. When the fighting resumed the 114th had been re-reinforced with the 9th Minnesota and the 93rd Indiana had resumed their position.

Meanwhile, several other Union Infantry divisions were engaged in skirmishes elsewhere in the Cross Roads vicinity. General Forrest demonstrated a far superior sense of battlefield strategy than Sturgis. Although outnumbered, Forrest easily exploited the fatigue and confusion of the Union force. It did not take long for most Union troops to turn in full retreat. They scurried back in the direction from whence they came; northwest toward Ripley, Mississippi. Of course some Unions troops remained steadfast in their resolve to defeat Forrest. First among these brave soldiers were the 114th Illinois and the 55th and 59th US Colored Infantries.

As we have seen by his letters home, Asa Newton Pascal was racist and condescending toward black people. Perhaps his attitude changed during the bloody battle at Brice's Cross Roads. We will never know. If he wrote any letters after his capture they have not survived. We can only guess that he must have been impressed by the valor of the former slaves.

While most of the white troops retreated, Col. Bouton's soldiers stood beside the 114th and covered the retreat. This is remarkable in face of the fact that Confederate soldiers seldom demonstrated mercy toward black Union soldiers. The palpable hatred between Forrest and the black Union troops was mutual and deep and it would play a role in the uncommon valor the black troops exhibited at Brice's Cross Roads. The black soldiers remembered Fort Pillow and they were determined to get their revenge.

Besides being abandoned by most of their fellow Union troops, the 114th and the US Colored Infantries were at the added disadvantage of being armed with old bayonet rifles, while many rebel soldiers fired at them with the more effective six-shooter. Col. McMillan later commented that all of the Union troops were dispirited, except the 114th Illinois. Apparently, he didn't find it necessary to credit the bravery of the black soldiers. The losses for the 55th and 59th were staggering. Nevertheless, even these brave troops finally came to the conclusion that they were involved in a lost cause. Col. McMillan began to order troops to retreat. The 114th never got the order. Soon they were the last Union regiment between Baldwin and Fulton Roads.

Under relentless fire the 114th slowly retreated, turning down Pontotoc Road. They halted several times to return fire, holding back most of the rebel troops and enabling the other Union troops to continue their retreat. Forrest would not allow an easy retreat. He gathered his troops for a final assault on the fleeing northern men. This allowed the 114th to escape across Tishimongo Creek and rejoin the Union force. Three miles beyond the creek General Sturgis ordered several infantries, including the 114th Illinois and 55th and 59th Colored Troops, to halt and prepare to deflect the pursuit. Eye witnesses reported seeing Sturgis and McMillan sharing a bottle of whiskey as they conferred.

The hodgepodge of Union soldiers turned to face their enemies one final time. Unable to locate supply wagons and nearly out of ammunition the men soon found themselves surrounded on three sides by screaming rebels. Now was the time to escape or be captured. In the case of the black soldiers it was escape or be murdered.

The road chosen for retreat was a scene of absolute chaos. Abandoned supply wagons, canons, ambulances, the dead, the dying, the dazed along with horses, dead and alive, and hordes of southern blacks hoping for refuge with the Union troops, all mingled in a mass of confusion. It was each man to himself. As darkness fell the weary and defeated soldiers found themselves on the mucky road toward Ripley but they would not stop for rest until their bodies gave out completely. Jubilant Confederate troops calmly and quietly followed their stricken foe, satisfied to wait until morning light to administer the final blow.

At dawn on June 11th the triumphant cavalry of Nathan Bedford Forrest raced through Ripley and beyond and everywhere they looked found the tattered remains of Union infantrymen that had marched out of Lafayette full of hope and vigor just ten days before. These men were now so defeated, so fatigued from the arduous march to find Forrest, the intense and bloody warfare that ensued and the frantic retreat through the night, that they no longer possessed the strength or the will to resist. Hundreds of Union soldiers became easy pickings for the prison camps.

It was probably at this time that Newton Paschal was captured and taken prisoner by Confederate forces. He may have been captured earlier, if wounded. We know that his cousin, Lt. Henry Freeman, Co. D, 114th Illinois, was captured in Ripley while he cared for a wounded officer. (See Letter to Mary Paschal from Henry Freeman, July 24, 1864).

Nearly 600 Union men were killed at Brice's Cross Roads compared to 140 Confederates. More than 1500 Union soldiers were taken prisoner. The 114th Illinois suffered heavy losses in the battle. 205 of the 397 members of the regiment engaged at the battle near Guntown were killed, wounded or taken prisoner. However, only ten members of the 114th actually died on the battlefield. Several others died later from wounds sustained in the battle; others were discharged due to disabilities from their wounds. Some members of the 114th were never accounted for after Brice's Cross Roads. Their remains were never recovered or they deserted during the chaos that followed. Most of the losses for the 114th came in the capture of prisoners by Forrest and his troops on June 11th.

Not all of the prisoners were sent to Andersonville. Some of them ended up at Confederate prisons in Wilmington, North Carolina; Florence, South Carolina or Millen, Georgia. One prisoner, Henry Gestring of Co. A, died from wounds while in transport to prison. At least one other, Lt. Freeman, escaped. The only other fatalities at Brice's Cross Roads for Co. A were Alvin French and Thomas Hickey, both of whom were killed in action.

General Forrest deserves credit for whipping a much larger army. Yet, it could be argued that a more astute Union commander would have defeated Forrest at Brice's Cross Roads. The lopsided defeat was an unnecessary and costly loss for the Union and a disgrace for General Sturgis, who was relieved of duty amid public outcry. For Asa Newton Paschal it was the beginning of the final and most gruesome chapter of his young life. Now a prisoner-of-war, Newton would spend the last two months of his life at Andersonville.

The Battle of Brice's Cross Roads remains one of the more obscure confrontations of the Civil War. Most books about the Civil War fail to mention this one-day carnage in Northern Mississippi. A small memorial now stands at the site of the battle near Guntown, Mississippi.

The main source for this information on the Battle of Brice's Cross Roads came from the definitive study of the battle: *Forrest at Brice's Cross Roads* by Edwin C. Bearss, copyright 1979, Press of Morningside Bookshop, Dayton, Ohio

Other sources:

Henry, Robert Selph, editor, *As They Saw Forrest*, copyright 1956, McCowat-Mercer Press, Inc., Jackson, Tennessee

Satterlee, John L. *The Journal and the 114th, 1861 to 1865*, copyright 1979. Phillips Brothers, Inc., Springfield, Illinois.

Wyeth, John Allen, *Life of General Nathan Bedford Forrest*, copyright 1975, Press of Morningside Bookshop, Dayton, Ohio

Additional information came from the *Adjutant General's Report* and from *Harper's History of the Great Rebellion.*

Letter to Mary Elizabeth Paschal from her Cousin, Lieutenant Henry D. Freeman, 114th Illinois Infantry, Company D

Memphis, Tennessee, July 24, 1864

Dear Cousin Mary: I have just received your letter of May 24. On the first of June, we started on a scout, we knew not where but supposed it would be only a few days until we would be back to our camp. But on account of having a drunken inefficient general to lead us, we met one of the most disastrous defeats of the war. Our whole train and all the artillery was captured and we lost in killed, wounded and prisoners some 1,500 or 2,000 men. I was detached to stay with our wounded and was found with them and of course taken prisoner. Some of our wounded was brought in ambulances 20 miles the night after the battle (10 June). It was found that it would be impossible to reach Memphis with the wounded and was thought best to stop them in Ripley, a small town some 85 miles S.E. of Memphis. It was their that I surrendered, it being the best that I could do at the time. Our forses was pursued by the enemy and a great many of them captured and some killed. Our wounded was all soon moved further south to what they call Lauderdale Springs,

*where they have extensive hospital arrangements. When
the wounded was moved, it was found that Col. McKeaig[177]
of the 120th Illinois Inf. Reg. could not be moved without
endangering his life so the Colonel was left in Ripley and I
was detailed to stay with him. I was their near 3 weeks until
our forces began to make demonstrations toward another
scout in that section. I was taken from Ripley on the 3rd of
July and on the 4th reached Tupelo, a point on the Mobile
& Charleston RR. Here I was kept 3 or 4 days when they
started me south again. We proceeded as far as Ocalina,
some 100 miles North of Meridian, Miss. the first day. The
next morning we were taken to the cars and shipped as they
supposed for Mobile. But I made my escape by jumping off
the cars while running at a speed of some 15 or 20 miles per
hour. I was 5½ days in the woods before I reached our lines.
In this expedition we lost 22 men killed and wounded. Our
company is now small, only reports 16 men. You spoke of not
having heard from your brother. He was with us on the expedition alluded to and was taken prisoner. This is all the news
I can collect concerning him at present. If I hear anything in
the future I will not fail to inform you of his whereabouts.
Hoping to hear from you soon, I must bring my present
epistle to a close with a wish that the sunlight of heaven may
ever shine along your pathway and that a kind providence
may so order affairs that we may meet again to relive the
privations of the past and the prospects of the future. May
heaven bless and protect you. Your cousin, H. D. Freeman I
will send you a kiss this time.*

---

177 Colonel George Washington McKeaig, of Shawneetown, Illinois, enlisted on October 29, 1862, and was mustered out on September 10, 1865.

Part Three

Andersonville and the Death of Pvt. Asa Newton Paschal

Photograph courtesy of the National Archives.

Photo of Andersonville Prison, taken only three days before the death of Newton Paschal.

Captured at Brice's Cross Roads, Asa Newton Paschal was taken to the Andersonville Prison near Americus, Georgia. It is not known if Newton sustained an injury during the battle but when one considers the ferocity of the encounter and the prominent role the 114th Illinois assumed, it seems likely that he did. An injury was not enough to earn a prisoner a reprieve from Andersonville.

The story of Andersonville is well known. It is one of the most infamous chapters of American history. The average American has been exposed to the brutal realities of Andersonville through numerous books and two television movies; Ken Burns epic documentary *The Civil War*, shown on Public Broadcasting Stations, and the TNT film *Andersonville*. Most of the Andersonville saga that has been told and retold relates to the events that transpired there during the fateful summer of 1864 when Newton was present.

Andersonville is the best known of the Civil War prison camps. It was by no means the only such camp. All other prisoner-of-war camps, both Union and Confederate, shared many of the inhumane conditions and high mortality rate of Andersonville. Nevertheless, while most camps stepped well beyond the line of human decency, Andersonville plunged into the abyss.

The Andersonville stockade opened on February 25, 1864. Prior to 1864 most prisoners-of-war in the Union and the Confederacy were simply exchanged one-for-one. When the war escalated to its unfathomable proportions prisoner exchange became difficult and impractical. Good faith efforts at exchange were wanting on both sides. The CSA did not want to release black soldiers and Secretary of War Edwin Stanton used that as a pretext to end all exchange; nor was rescuing a top concern. General Sherman, who was burning his way through the heart of Dixie, did not attempt to free the prisoners of Andersonville. Sadly, the prisoners who dared to hope spoke of little else.

Andersonville was built to accommodate the swelling numbers of Union soldiers captured by Confederate troops during battles and raids. The stockade's original dimensions of approximately 1000 ft. by 800 ft. were intended to house 10,000 prisoners. By mid-summer of 1864 over 30,000 men were imprisoned there. These cramped quarters were further reduced by the deadline, an area near the stockade walls off-limits to prisoners, and by the large swamp that covered most of the middle ground within the prison. The length of the stockade was enlarged to about 1600 feet in August of 1864 but it did little to alleviate the overcrowding, especially since the expansion came at a time when hundreds of new prisoners were arriving daily.

The prison offered nothing in the way of comforts for its captives. The men had nothing except that which they carried with them upon arrival at Andersonville and that was usually nothing more than the clothes on their bodies. There were no trees, shrubs or grasses left in the Andersonville compound by the summer of 1864. The ground on which the prisoners slept was swarming with maggots, lice, and other parasitic vermin. They lived off the excrement that was to be found everywhere. They also lived off the decaying flesh and organs of dying men, and in the meager food rations that came into the camp on the very same wagons that took out the dead.

Newton Paschal arrived at Andersonville in mid-June 1864. He couldn't have picked a worse time. The rains were steady and the camp was a quagmire of mud and human waste. He arrived by train from Mississippi, probably via Mobile. His little brother Tommy, ironically, would take part in the siege of Mobile nine months later. The train cars stopped about a quarter of a mile from the camp and the prisoners would take the final distance by foot. One in four would never walk out.

New arrivals would be "welcomed" by Captain Henry Wirz, before entering the camp. Wirz, a Swiss immigrant, was not technically in charge of Andersonville, although he is remembered as the commander of the prison. That distinction actually belongs to General John H. Winder, who came from a noted American military family. Winder apparently attempted, on several occasions, to improve the conditions at Andersonville. He constantly ran into obstacles. Meanwhile, Wirz ran the day-to-day operations of the camp and subsequently took the blame for its disgraceful conditions.

Numerous eyewitnesses have meticulously described Captain Wirz, who was born in Zurich, Switzerland in 1823 and emigrated to America in 1849. Some of the accounts, mostly from sympathetic southerners, have portrayed a brave and fair man who was simply trying to carry out an impossible order. Northerners recalled Wirz as angry, arrogant and mean-spirited. Many of the prisoners found his strutting mannerisms and thick accent to be almost a comic relief from their dire circumstances.

Once inside the gates Newton and his fellow captives from Brice's Cross Roads may well have been given a second inauspicious welcoming from a gang of prison thugs and thieves known as the " Raiders". As Newton and the other "fresh fish" gawked in fear and disbelief at the sea of misery before them, the Raiders would jump them and steal everything of value. Resistance would be met with savage violence.

Newton and his friends from the 114th would not have to deal with the Raiders for long. On the third of July fellow Illinois soldiers, most notably Pvt. Leroy Key of the 16th Illinois Cavalry and a colorful member of the 67th Illinois Infantry who went by the name of Limber Jim, led a prison uprising against the Raiders. For the main prison population it was a chance to strike back at some of their oppressors and the hapless Raiders took the full brunt of their pent-up fury. The blows against the Raiders were also blows against Wirz, his rebel guards, and the whole injustice of such inhumane conditions.

After a thorough beating the Raiders were bound and gagged and handed over to Wirz who, to his credit, agreed to confine them away from the general prison population until their peers could arrange a trial and carry out a punishment. On July 11, 1865, Wirz returned the Raiders to the prison where several were forced to run a gauntlet of angry fellow prisoners and six were executed by hanging. It was an extraordinary event that put an end to the rampant gang activity at Andersonville and the entire historic episode was undoubtedly witnessed by Newton. Yet while revenge might have been sweet, the gruesome execution of the Raiders (four of them were slowly strangled to death at the end of poorly constructed nooses) did little to lessen the intense suffering that grew with each new day throughout July and August.

Another noted event in the history of Andersonville occurred during Newton's time there. On August 12, 1864, just eight days before Newton's death, a "miracle" gave hope and renewed spiritual faith to many prisoners. Following a particularly hard rain, dirt near a stockade wall was washed away and a long suppressed spring burst forth with fresh, clean water. The prisoners called it Providence Springs, and took it as a sign that God had not forsaken them.

Also during Newton's imprisonment the photographer Andrew Jackson Riddle arrived at Andersonville and snapped the only known photographs of the hellish prison camp. Could Newton be among the sea of anguished and resigned faces looking up at Riddle in one of his most famous photographs? We may never know, though it is entirely possible.

By the time Newton arrived the population of the prison had outpaced the availability, or willingness of the CSA to make available, even the most meager of rations. The kitchens could not possibly cook rations for 30,000 starving men even if the food was available. On many days during the summer of 1864 no rations were issued to the men at Andersonville. When rations were issued they were typically uncooked. The prisoners were told to cook their own food and yet, with a scarcity of wood, this was seldom possible, especially for the newer prisoners. Consequently, food was often eaten raw.

The rations usually consisted of nothing more than ground corn (cob included), which the men called "Indian Meal", beans or rice. Occasionally the men would get a pinch of salt or a slice of raw meat. Of course, all food was infested with maggots and other worms. The prisoners became accustomed to this and rarely picked them out. Cornmeal was usually mixed with water to make bread or mush. Unfortunately, most of the water at Andersonville was dangerously polluted with grease from the kitchen, soap from the Confederate camps upstream and fecal matter from the prisoners. The open pit latrine, so vividly photographed by Riddle with sick men sitting on the crude benches, was situated right next to the water source. Needless to say the high mortality rate at Andersonville was due largely to malnutrition, starvation or gastrointestinal related diseases such as chronic diarrhea. Most prisoners also suffered from scurvy.

Too weak to move, many men suffered severe sunburn as temperatures exceeded 100 degrees on a regular basis during the months of July and August. Many of the weakest men lay upon the filthy ground, exposed to the searing rays of the southern sun, unable to gain shelter. As they rotted on the inside they literally baked on the outside. Hundreds of men died in this fashion during the summer of 1864.

The first-person accounts of Andersonville are numerous and horrifying. It was without doubt an American concentration camp. More than 30,000 men lived to testify to its horrors. Many visitors to the prison, including many southerners, confirmed the grotesque details. One of the most damning accounts came from the Confederate Inspector General during a visit to the camp that coincided with Newton's first days at Andersonville. Suffice to say that for Newton Paschal the simple tranquility of farm life near Beardstown, Illinois might as well have been a million miles away. Andersonville was a world beyond the realm of imagination for a man of 19th century rural America.

Newton survived the prison for two months. He died on August 20, 1864. The cause of death was listed as chronic diarrhea. A modern autopsy would have listed a litany of afflictions. He was 26 years old. His death was certainly slow, horrible and excruciating; despite the best efforts of his fellows from the 114th to comfort him. He was buried

Photograph by Chloe Fulton.

The grave of Asa Newton Paschal at the Andersonville National Historic Site. His name is misspelled as J.M. Pashall. The National Parks Service is in the process of correcting the error.

under grave 6301 and, in one final indignity, his name was misspelled as JM Pashall. He was not the first soldier from Illinois to perish at Andersonville. Corporal M.R. Kell of the 49th Illinois died of smallpox at Andersonville just ten days after the prison opened. Eventually, the prison would claim over 900 men from Illinois, nearly 10% of the all the Union soldiers who died there during its 13 months of operation. 155 men from Illinois died at Andersonville during the month of August, 1864. On the day that Newton died, seven other men from Illinois joined him in the death house.

Newton was the first member of the 114th to die at Andersonville. At least three more would follow; Patrick Smith of Co. H on Oct. 15, 1864 (grave #10975), Robert Clark of Co. F on Feb. 18, 1965 (grave # 12672), and William Penny of Co. F on Feb. 26, 1865 (grave # 12707). Andersonville records show an I. Gordon of Co. B, dying on April 25, 1865 (grave # 12847), 16 days after Lee surrendered to Grant and eleven days after the assassination of Abraham Lincoln. This death is a mystery. There was a Joel Gordon from Company B listed as "missing" after the Battle of Brice's Cross Roads, but the Adjutant General's Report shows Joel Gordon as being mustered out of service on August 3, 1865.

The Andersonville Prison is now a National Historic Site. What happened there continues to be the topic of heated discussion between Civil War buffs and historians. There continues to be apologists for Wirz and other Confederate officers and soldiers who have been blamed for the atrocities at Andersonville. Some argue that it was the USA and not the CSA that bore the responsibility for what transpired behind those pine log walls. An Internet web site, CSAnet, attempts to portray Henry Wirz as a misunderstood hero who was unjustly executed for war crimes. The site also contends that "slavery was not racist."

In fact, Wirz was the only Confederate officer that paid for the crimes of Andersonville with his life. Unlike the amateurish execution of the Raiders, Wirz was strangled to death by an improperly placed noose that was almost certainly intentional. It is easy to imagine that his execution proved little consolation for the families of the 12,912 Union soldiers who perished under his watch.

Sources:

Futch, Ovid L., *The History of Andersonville Prison*, copyright 1968, University of Florida Press

Guernsey, Alfred H. and Alden, Henry M., *Harper's Pictorial History of the Civil War*, copyright 1866, The Fairfax Press, New York

Goss, Warren Lee, *The Soldier's Story of His Captivity at Andersonville*, copyright 1871, I.N. Richardson & Co., Boston

Hicken, Victor, *Illinois in the Civil War*, copyright 1966, University of Illinois Press, Urbana & London

McElroy, John, *This Was Andersonville*, copyright 1957, McDowell, Obolensky Inc., New York

Ripple, Ezra Hoyt, (Edited by Mark Snell), *Dancing Along the Deadline, An Andersonville Memoir of a Prisoner of the Confederacy*, copyright 1996, Presidio Press, Novato, California

Roberts, Edward F. *Andersonville Journey, The Civil War's Greatest Tragedy*, copyright 1998, Burd Street Press, Shippensburg, PA

Van, Brig. Gen. J.W., *Report of the Adjutant General of the State of Illinois*, 1866, Springfield, Illinois

Part Four

The Letters of

Pvt. Samuel Thomas Paschal,
Company F, 47th Illinois Infantry

Samuel Thomas Paschal.

Asa Newton Paschal called him "Tommy" or "Blake." He was 16 years old when he enlisted at Beardstown, Illinois on March 3, 1865, in the 47th Illinois Infantry, Company F. Except for one letter to his sister, Rachel, all of his surviving letters were written to his sister, Mary Elizabeth Paschal Hobson.

It is not hard to imagine a 16 year-old Tommy, still angry about the loss of his brother Newton and wanting to avenge his brother's death. Tommy was an orphan when he enlisted. He was cared for by his sister Mary, the next youngest child in the family but still six years his senior. Mary was devastated by the loss of Newton and it is unlikely that she approved of Tommy's enlistment.

The company that Tommy joined was a consolidated unit that included only five other boys from Beardstown. The new company was almost immediately sent off to Mobile, Alabama where they would engage in what became known as the Confederate's last stand. The fresh recruits camped on beautiful Dauphin Island, south of Mobile in the Gulf of Mexico. Fort Gaines, a remnant of the War of 1812, was located on the island.

The new boys of the 47th Illinois were ill-equiped and unprepared for battle. They drilled with hickory sticks until they received rifles. They spent much of their leisure time exploring the island and harvesting oysters. This must have been a fantastic delicacy for the farmboys from Illinois. They ate oysters morning, noon and night until they became sick of them.

Unlike his brother Newton, Tommy would not have to wait long for action. Within three weeks of arrival in Alabama Tommy joined his fellow soldiers from the 47th Illinois in the siege of Mobile. He must have been excited to hear that his brother's old unit, the 114th Illinois, was also part of the force under the command of Major General Edward Canby.

From the relative comfort of Dauphin Island the boys of the 47th Illinois moved north along Mobile Bay and were engaged in the quick and decisive attacks on Spanish Fort and Fort Blakely, about ten miles east of the city of Mobile. The forts had been defended by the ragged remnants of John Bell Hood's Army of the Tennessee, which after losing 23,500 killed, wounded or missing on the western front, regrouped for one final, and somewhat sad and pathetic stand in Mobile. It would prove to be the last stand of the entire Confederacy. On April 9, 1865, Robert E. Lee had surrendered to Ulysses S. Grant at Appomatax Courthouse in Virginia. This effectively ended the Civil War, but word did not reach Mobile for several days. Spanish Fort fell on April 8th and the next day Fort Blakely, along the Tensas River, was routed by Union troops. Tommy was there, but he and his fellow soldiers could not have know that the battles they had just fought in were unnecessary.

April the 10th, 1865, Camp Near Blakely, Alabama

Dear Sister: It is with pleasure I sit down this morning to write you a few lines to let you know that I am well at presant and hope that you are the same. Mary, the news is good down here. Nite before last Fort Spanish evaskcuated[178], 200 and fifty 8 men came out with the flag of truc and gave them rifoes up, and we took about 300 hundred prisnors besides. Then next morning we had marching orders and we marcht about three miles and pitched our tents. Then last nite thare

---

178 Spanish Fort, outside Mobile, Alabama, came under heavy bombardment by Union forces on the afternoon of April 8, 1865, and during that night, the Confederates evacuated the Fort.

*was a charge made on Blakely[179] and took it and from 15
hundred to two thousand prisoners and to Rebel generels and
the next thing we will have Mobile I think, and it is reported
that Grant is in Richmond[180] and I hope it is so. If things goes
in like they have here latey I think this war will be over prety
soon. I received a letter from Rachel last weak. I havant had
but two letters from home sence I left nor I havant wrote but
few for I havant had much chance for we have bin moving
ever sence we left Camp Butler. All of us that left Beardstown
got along first rate except Ben Harres[181] and we left him at
Cairo sick and we havant heard from him sence but we are
looking for him ever day. Sol Sills[182] and George White
was over to see us the other day and they sade that Henry
Freeman and them boys was all well. I would a went over
to the 114th[183] but thare was so meny Rebels that it was
dangerous to go out thru the timber. I beleave that I have
wrote all the news at present. Writ soon and give me all the
news. I will wind up by saying hurrah for the union. So no
more at present. Yours truley, Thomas. To Miss Mary Paschal,
Derect your letters to Thomas Paschal, the 47 Reg Ill Vol,
Cairo, Illinois*

On April 12th the 47th Illinois marched north toward Montogomery
and arrived there on April 24th. Union forces under the command
of General James H. Wilson had already subdued the area. The 47th
Illinois would remain in Alabama as part of the peace-keeping force.

---

179 Fort Blakely was attacked by the combined Federal forces on April 9, 1865. It fell
without heavy losses.

180 Robert E. Lee had surrendered to Ulysses S. Grant on April 9, 1865.

181 Benjamin J. Harris enlisted with the 47th Ill, Co. F, on March 3, 1865, from Beardstown, Illinois. He died at Cairo, Illinois on March 31, 1865.

182 Solomon Sills (114th Illinois, Co. A) (*Sills)

183 "On March 23, [the 114th] embarked on a steamer at Lake Pontchartrain for Spanish Fort, Alabama, and was engaged during the siege at Spanish Fort." *Adjutant
General's Report.*

Besides Montgomery, the boys of the 47th camped in Selma, Cahaba, Demopolis and Camden, Alabama.

Apparently Tommy Paschal did not find time to write home between April 10th and May 2nd when he certainly heard the big news from Virginia and Washington D.C. Therefore we do not have an account of Tommy's feelings regarding the successful conclusion for the war for the Union, nor of the assassination of Abraham Lincoln.

Two days after the following letter was written, General Richard Taylor of the CSA, the son of former U.S. president Zachary Taylor, officially surrendered the western troops of the Confederate army to General Edward Canby in Citronelle, Alabama.

May the 2nd, 1865, Camp Near Montgomery, Alabama

Dear Sister Mary: It is with pleasure I sit down this morning to let you know that I am well at presant and hope that you are the same. We have bin on a march since I wrote last. We marcht 13 days and we got in Camp last Tuesday and I would write sooner but thare was no male going north till yesterday and then I had to go on guard and couldent write then. I receved your letter dated March the 26 the day before we started and we was under marching orders. Then not noing what time we would start, I dident anser it then and I havnt had eny chanse till now. You wanted to no wethir the first boys that left town first was all together or not. We are all in the 47 Ill Co. F., A. J. Smiths[184] gurilers, 16th Army Corps, and Camp life I like firstrate. I can just make as good coffie as the most of them. While I was on guard I think thare was as meny as 50 rebs came along my post from Lee's army and I talked to a good meney of them. Some hated to come out and say that they was whipt. They would say that they allways thought that they would whip the yanks. When

---

184 Brigadier General Andrew Jackson Smith (1815-1897) from Pennsylvania was the commander of the 16th Corps, Department of the South, at the time of this letter. Thomas' word "gurilers" is guerrillas.

you write next I want you to write the news for we heare every thing hare and never knoe when to beleve every thing. Will wrout that he had a larger family than when I left.[185] Tell him I want to know what his daughters name is. Tell them to give it a pety name fur I think it must be good looking if it looks eney [like] its dad an mam. Tell Rachel that I will write to her next weak if we are in Camp. All you folks thare at home must excuse me for not wrighting oftener for I havent much chance. When we get some where we know we will stay I will write regular. So no more at present. Yours truley, Thomas Paschal To Miss Mary Paschal

May the 7th, 1865

Dear Sister Mary: We received male this evning and I received two letters from you and one from sister Maggie. They was all well. I was very glad to here from you and Maggie. We have sad news. Capt Leiks[186] received a letter stating that Benson Harris was dead. He died the 31st of March. He was not well when he started from Camp Butler[187] but he felt better the day we left and when we got to Cario he was sent to the hospitel. Burns[188] and Cotrell[189] went to see him and he sade that he was better and then we left and never heard from him till we heard that he was dead. I was very sory when the news came. I will quit for this time.

Yours forever, Thomas Paschal To Miss Mary Paschal

---

185 Harriett Ellen Paschal, daughter of William H. and Emlin (Dunn) Paschal, was born March 25, 1865, and named in honor of William's deceased sister, Harriet Paschal Skinner.

186 Captain Phillip S. Likes (Co. F, 47th Illinois).

187 Camp Butler is where Thomas and Newton both received their military training.

188 Charles E. Burns (Co. F, 47th Regiment) (*Burns)

189 Abel F. Cottrel (Co. F, 47th Regiment) to whom Thomas referred to as "Dock." (*Cottrel)

May the 7th, 1865, Camp near Montgomery, Alabama

Mary, I will wright you a few lines to you. Rlighier[190] you wrote as tho you thought that I didn't wright to you often anof but I have wrote more to you than eney one else. I gave Rachel the decription of our house or else I would give it to you. Camp is very still to day for it is a day of prar and thanksgivng. When you wright give me all the news and tell me how _____[191] gits along and the rest of the famely. I will put som Rebel scrip in here for Eddie and Johnne[192]. Some of the boys are making grate calculations to come home prety soon but I dont know wether they are mistaken or not. For my part I dont care for this sutes me beter than eney thing that I hav found to do latley.

No more at presant. Yours forever, Thomas Paschal

May the 14th, 1865, Near Selma, Alabama[193]

Dear Sister Mary. It is with pleasure I sit to wright you a few lines to let you know that I am well at presant and hope that you are the same. We started from Montomery last Wendsday and arived here to day. It is Sunday. We expect to take the trane in the morning where for I can not tell but when we get to camp I will wright agane. Mary, I dont want you to be uneasy about me for thare is no use of it. I am glad that we are agoing to wride on the cars for I despise wriding on the boats.

---

190 Earlier

191 This word looks like "snip" or "smith" but one cannot be sure.

192 Eddie and Jonnie were sons of Thomas' sister, Rachel Paschal Peters. Jonnie Peters was born November 20, 1857, and died November 13, 1869, at about 12 years old; Eddie Peters was born October 27, 1853, and died on May 24, 1873, at 19 years.

193 This letter was written on stationery provided to the soldiers by The United States Christian Commission. The letterhead reads "The United States Christian Commission sends this sheet as the Soldier's messenger to his Home. Let it hasten to those who wait for tidings."

I can not tell when I will come home but I dont have eney idah of staying my time out. I havant time to wright mutch for the post master is here. I am ansering your letters up to the 16th of April. Mary, I think that I get your letters regular and I dont know what is the reason you dont get my letters for I have wrote a good meney. Wright soon and give me all the news.

I remain your affectionate brother, Thomas Paschal Co F 47 Ill, To Miss Mary Paschal. PS. Tell all the girls that I am all wright. Thare is some tolrable pety girls down here but thare aint none that can come up with the Illinois girls.

May the 21st, 1865, Demopolis, Alabama

Dear Sister Mary: It is with pleasure I sit down this Sunday evening to let you no that I am well at presant and hope that you are the same. Mary, we have got stopt at last. We have got nice barracks to live in here. Our boys and the rebs are all together and the muscueters[194] are our worst enemy now and there is tolrable hevy skermishing and bayonet charge. Some nites there loses is hevey. I havent much news to wright. Tom Burns was here yesterday to see Charley and I think that he is considrable rebel but he is in the US Commisary Department now. Mary, you must excues this sheat of paper for it is my last and I dont no when I can get eney more for greenbacks is played out in our Company. If you dont get eney more letters from me you must onley think that I hant got eney more paper. Dock Cotrell is in the printing office in this town now.[195] He went yesterday. How long he will stay I cant say. We hant had eney male for two weeks. I heard that it was at Vixburg.[196] I supose if we stay here long it will come on. I dont think

---

194 mosquitoes

195 Abel "Dock" Cottrel was a printer by trade. (*Cottrel)

196 Mail must have been misrouted to Vicksburg, Mississippi.

that I like souldering hardley well anofe to go in the regular service so you need not be ancuses about that at all. Mary, I will wright agane as soon as I can get eney more paper. I think that I will be up in Illinois prety soon if all reports is true. News is now that the 16 Corps is to be musterd out as soon as things can be arranged but I dont know how true it is. Wright soon and give me all the news, so no more at presant.

Yours truley, Thomas Paschal PS. Give my love all enquiring friends and keep a large porshin for yourself.

May the 25th, 1865, Demopolis, Alabama

Dear Sister Mary: It is with pleasure I take my pen in hand to inform you that I am well and hope that you are the same. Your letter came safe to hand dated April the 30. I was glad to here from home and that things was geting along well. You sade that Bennys folks had not heard from him sence he left Camp Butler. We left him at Cairo sick and he died thare but I supose that you have heard about him before now for I have writen about his death in ever letter that I have wrote sence I heard of his death. All so Able Cotrell wrote to his mother. Mary, we have a nice place to camp, good water and everthing is lovely and the goose hangs hy. I heard that the 114th Illinois was musterd out[197] and I hope that it is so for when I get home I want to see all the boys. Our old Colonel has got ten dollers and a fine pair of boots bet on being [out by] the forth of July but I am a little afraid that he is a little to fast. I think that if nothing hapens we will be home in time for the fair next fall. we dont have much news in camp now. McCandless[198] got a

---

197 "After the surrender of Mobile, the [114th] Regiment marched to Montgomery, Alabama, arriving April 24th, and bridging the Alabama River with pontoons, remained on duty at the bridge until July 17th, when it was ordered to Vicksburg, Mississippi, for muster-out." Adjutant General's Report.

198 DeWitt C. McCandless (Co. F, 47th Regiment) (*McCandless)

paper from Beardstown stating that Spanish Fort was taken but I think that I new about as much about it as the papers did. Time passes off very fast. I have bin in prety near one forth of my time and it dont seam long. I just imagin that I can see the farmers plowing and planting corn while I can lay around Camp [and] have nothing to do much. I only come on duty about once a weak. I will haft to go on drill very soon for our Captan haft to take the bugllers out on dress parade this evening so we haft to put on a little more stile than comon. We had a nice time on dress parade last evening. The band came out playing the girl I left behind me. It made me think of old Cass Co. You wanted me to send you some curiosity or other. I dont know of eney unless I could send you a darkey and I guess I wont send you one of them for I dont want eney of them up thare. This paper wrights mighty nice for I got it by the slight of hand. Tell Eddie that he must take mighty good care of that little colt and have it nice and fat whin I get home. The band is over here in the grove playing the tune we will wralley rond the brave old flag that bares the stripes and stars. There, they have started another tune. It is thare is good care in youthfall age. There they have started up yankee doodle. I guess I will quit wrighting tunes. I think that I have wrote a large letter this time wether it is intresting one or not. When you wright agane give all the news and how all the good looking girls gets along and how is Wm family and Joes and Rachels and all the rest off the folks in general. I will send you ten dollers of rebel money. I dont know wether you have seene eney of it or not. It is playd out is the reason it is cut up so. All the rest of the boys is well that left when I did. I will quit for this time. Pleas excues all bad wrighting and wright when ever you feel like it and I will do the same. Thomas Paschal To Miss Mary Paschal

June 9, 1865, Demopolis, Alabama

Dear Sister Mary. It is with pleasure I will try to anser your kind letter of May 22. I think that I get all of your letters. I cant tell what is the reason you dont get my letters for I have ritten a good meney and you wrote that you had not received but one from me yet. I am well this morning. The helth of the Company is tolrable good. You have bin wrighting that you was looking for me home but you need not look for me till you see me a comeing. I have heard that we would be musterd out the 18 of this month but I can not tell how true it is. My idah[199] is that I will be home in time to take up winter quarters but some of the men in our Co wants to go home perty tolrable bad. I would not mind beang home a little while to see how things gets along but I like this better than farming. There are three Reg at this place and two of them is geting payed off to day but the old 47 dont get payed this time. I cant think of much to wright for thres is no news of eney importence. Oh yes I like to a forgot to tell you that T. J. Burns[200] was married last nite and Charles E. Burns went to the wedding and has not yet got back yet.

Pleas excues all bad wrighting and spelling. I remain your afectionate brother, Thomas Paschal Co F 47 Reg To Miss Mary Paschal

June 17, 1864, Demopolis, Alabama

Dear Sister Mary: It is with pleasure I will try to anser your kind letter which I receved yesterday dated of May 30, 15 days on the road I was glad to here from you and that you was all well. I am well at presant and hope that this will

---

199 idea

200 Thomas J. Burns (*Burns)

arrive safe and find you all the same. I received a letter from Joe the other day and sent one back to him wether it gets thare of not. You apear to think that you dont get letters anofe from me but I think that I wright often anofe for you to get one allmost every weak wether thay get thare or not. I allso received a letter from sister Margret last week. They was all well then. Sister, you send stamps enofe for me to anser your letters but I would like for you to send me 25 cents of stamps in your next letter if you please and I will try to get paper and envelops down hear all tho I havant got a cent of money nor hant had for some time nor I would not care if I had enof to by paper. Your letters apear to come very regular to me. Mabe you had better send me a dolar or too. If you hant got some money of mine, go to Mr. Leonards[201] and get enof for you to bye all the close you want[202]. If you dident get eney school you must do just as you please and enjoy yourself as well as you can and you can get along as long as I have eney thing. By the way you wrout and the most of the letters that the souldiers gets talks like they were looking for us home eney day but mabe that they will haft to look a good while and maby not long. I cant tell nothing a bout it at presant for we dont get eney papers down here in this out away place. I think that I will be thare in time for the fare and mabie not that soon. I am glad that Charlie is going to get home so soon. I am afraid that he will beat me home badley but I cant help that. I guess that I must wind up for this time. Yours truley, Thomas Paschal Co F 47 To Miss Mary Paschal. Wright when you pleas and I will do the same if posoble. We have been here over a month and I dont no how much longer we will stay here. Goodbye Sister Mollie[203]

---

201 James C. Leonard owned the bank in Beardstown, Illinois.

202 Thomas is telling Mary to buy clothes for herself.

203 Thomas sometimes refers to Mary by the nickname "Mollie"

June 22, 1865, Demopolis, Alabama

Dear Sister Mary: It is with pleasure I will anser your kind letter which I received about a half an hour ago. All so received one from Sister Rachel. Yours was dated June the 7 and hers the 9. I was glad to here from home and that you was all well. I am well at presant and hope that this will find you the same. We have bin here 5 weaks and I dont know how much longer we will stay. We may not stay hare a weak and maby we will stay for months. I am glad that Thanel[204] thinks he will be home by the 4th of July. I say if he gets home by that time he is a going to beat me badley but I cant help that. I am coming home when I am musterd out and I dont know when that will be. Some time betwean now & next March I think. Well thare ant much news here of much importence. We have a nice house to live in, plenty to eat. Dress parade is playd out & we have Co. drill once a day and I onely come on duty once a weak & that ant much to what I had to do at Spanish Fort. I was on duty thare every other nite diging rifle pits and planting canons but that was a good while ago. I can just imagen I can see the farmers at work while I am down here havin the gayest old time you ever saw. I like this better than farmen eney how. I received 25 cents in your letter and I dont know hardley what to bye with it. I think that I will bye a scane[205] of thread. I would bye paper and envelops with it but it would get such little I guess I will wate and see if you wont send some more. I have writen all that I can think off at presant so no more. Yours truley, T. P. PS. Write soon and give me all the news. Mr. Thomas Paschal, Co F 47 Reg Vol. to Miss Mary E. Paschal

---

204 Refers to Nathaniel Peters, husband of his sister, Rachel. Peters was drafted into Co. E, Illinois 36th Infantry on Sept. 30, 1864, and mustered out on June 15, 1865.

205 Skein of thread.

June 27, A.D., 1865, Demopolis Alabama

Dear Sister Mary: It is with pleasure that I will try to anser your kind letter dated June the 13 and was glad to here from you and that you was all well. I am well and hope that this will find you all the same. Mary, it will be the 4th of July down here prety soon and I expect it will up thare and you must enjoy your self the best that you can and I will do the same. It will be the first forth I have spent in Alabama and I think it will be the last. Mary, when I come home I think that I will bring my gun and equipments. I can get them for 6 dollars and then you can see how they look in Dixey . We left the 114 Reg at Montgomery the 10 of May and I havent saw eney of them since. I suppose that they are thare yet if they havant left dont you. Mary, I am almost as misheveous as I use to be. I expect if I could get to see some of them northern gerls I would see all these Sothern Rebs gerls aint eney acount at all. Mary, I cant be thare the forth of July but when I do get home I will have a gay time you had better reckon. Sister, I get along in this Company as well as if I had bin in a company that I know all the boys.[206] Thare is some as good boys in this Co as I ever sean. Some of the boys are drawing new close[207] to day but I have anofe at presant. I beleave that I have writen all that I can think off at presant, so no more. Yours truley, Thomas Paschal

July 8th, 1865, Demopolis, Alabama

Dear Sister Mary: It is with pleasure I will try to anser your kind letter June the 21 and was glad to hear that you was all

---

206 In Thomas' Company F, only six men came from his hometown of Beardstown, Illinois – Abel Cottrel, Charles Burns, Benjamin Harris, DeWitt McCandless, Woodson Sills and himself.

207 Clothes

well. I am the same and hope that this will find you all wright.
I was very glad indead to hear that Thanel had got home
all wright. Tell him that I am mutch obliged to him for his
kindness sending me those stamps and greenbacks for I was
almost out. Tell him to wright an tell me all the news and how
he liked the servis. He got home before I did but he started
some time before I did. I dont think that I wil haft to serve
eney longer than he did. All the boys are well that is in Camp.
Cotrell is printing in this place. Burns is on safe guard in the
country. We cant tell eney thing about when we leave hear I
have an idea that we will leave here before next month eney
how. You sade that you expected sister Maggie over to see you
and likley you would go home with her. I will wright to her to
day or tomorow. I guess you will see that I have my favoright
color for ink[208]. You may think that I cut my finger but that
is a mustake. Thare is some ink I own here in the wilderness.
I expect that I ought to wright Will a letter but he never had
eney thing to say hardley and it peared to me that I could not
think of eney thing to wright to him but I will do the best that
I can some of these days. This is Monday and I expect that
the farmers are harvesting up thare. If I was up there I dont
think that I could do a days work in a weak. I am about as
lazzie as I ever get to be but I cant help it. We havent eney
thing to do hardley. We have a little provost duty to do but
we dont come on more than once a weak and you know that
ant much or Thanel will tell you so, to the side of some that he
has done I expect, but I don't know what kind of a time he has
had, but we have had a firstrate time sence we left the sivilized
country[209]. Mary, this is a very good place for them that likes it
but it is most to warm for to suit me. I would like to be thare
to morow and have a nice time in the old City, but I will have
as good a time as the most of them for my chance. I must quit

---

208 This letter was written with red ink.

209 By "civilized country," he may be referring to Illinois or the Union states.

for this time. Pleas excuse all bad wrighting and spell. So no more at presant. Yours forever, Thomas Paschal. To Miss Mary E Paschal. PS Give my love to all enquiring friends and keep a good porshen for yourself.

July 9th, 1865, Demopolis, Alabama

Dear Sister: It is with pleasure that I sit down this evening to anser your kind letter which I recived yesterday dated June 26th and was glad to hear that you was well. I am well and hope that this this will find you the same. I was glad that you had got a school[210] and had so meney scholers for to start on and hope that they will keep coming & that you will keep haven an intresting school & enjoy your self the best that you can. I hope that I will be home in time to come after you when your time is out, but I can content my self down hear till spring if they say so but I would like to know something about it. We are here not noing when we will haft to leave. If they would tell us that we had to stay till spring then I would no what to do and would fix up and be as happy as a coon. I have some noshen of going out in the country as a safeguard but dont know wether I will or not yet. If I did I would only get my letters once a weak. It would be about 15 miles from camp and I should not come in very often. If I go I wood have nothing to do but eat and sleep and see that the negroes works well for they wont mind there masters[211] very well down here sence the souldiers came here but they are mighty fraid of the yankeys as they call us. I have received some 25 letters sence I left home. Mary, thare are plenty of peaches hear but as we dont draw

---

210 Mary taught at the Green Meadow School in Morgan County, Illinois.

211 Amid pandemonium, Congress had passed the 13th Amendment to the Constitution, prohibiting slavery throughout the United States, in January of 1865, but the required ratification by 27 states was not received until December, 1865, conferring upon Congress the power to enforce the Amendment.

*eney flouer we dont make eney coblers but do have them stewd
and they eat fistrate. I beleave that I have writen all the news
so I will quit. Pleas excuse all bad writen and spelling. No
more at presant. Yours forever, Thomas Paschal To Miss Mary
E Paschal. PS Give my love to Hazen and Birney[212]*

July 27th, 1865, Selma, Alabama

*Dear Sister: It is with pleasure that I sit down this morning
to anser your kind letter dated 13th. It found me well and I
hope that this will find you the same. I have nothing of importence to rite at this time. I am getting along finely. I like this
business very well but I ant a going to stay in the surves eney
longer than I can get out. It is very warm in this section of
Dallas kounty. I would like to be farther north at this time of
year. I expect that they will keep us down hear thru the warm
weather and when it gets cold they will send us further north.
I cant tell how long we will stay hear. I received a letter from
brother Joseph also this morning. They was all well and he
sayed that he was apponted my guardian[213] and that he had
made out the papers for brother Newtons back pay. I am glad
that your getting along so well with your school and have such
a nice time. I will quit for the presant. Yours forever, Thomas
Paschal To Miss Mary Paschal*

August 4th, 1865, Selma, Alabama

*Dear Sister: It is with pleasure that I will try to anser your
letters dated 19th & 25 of July which I received last nite and*

---

212 Hazen Skinner, husband of his late sister, Harriett, and Albert, their son, to whom
he refers as "Birney"

213 Since Thomas was only 17 years old and since his father, Coleman Paschal, had
died in April of 1852 and his mother, Sarah Street Paschal, in December of 1863,
the court appointed his oldest brother, Joseph, as his guardian.

was glad to hear from you and that you was well. I am tolrable
well at this time and hope that this will find you in good helth.
I have nothing of importence to wright at this time. I am glad
that you have such a large school and like it so well. If it was
not for you, Mary, I would not get eney letters at all hardley. I
get one from Rachel once a month. I have got 2 from Joe and
one [from] Will sence I have bin the serves. I dont know how
meney that I have received from [you]. I think about 20. I
have bin in the serves 5 months and the governmant has not
pade me a cent yet. It owes me something like one houndred &
thirty three & 3 cents. If it dont pay me some prety soon I will
think that it is kinder slow pay. Mabe it is all for the best for
I will have more when I am musterd out but I cant tell when
that will be, not a grate while tho I hope. Thare has bin a good
meney peaches hear this year but they are all most gon now.
Thare ant a grate meney appels in this county. Please excues
all bad writing & spelling, also this poor letter. I remain your
afectionate Brother, Thomas Paschal To Miss Mary E Paschal

On the back of the August 4th letter above, Mary Paschal wrote that
she had received this letter on August 19, and then wrote, "August 20,
1865. One year ago my noble soldier Brother Newton died away down
in Georgia at the Anderson prison. My Dear Brother how he must have
suffered. Starved to death by Devils in mens clothing. For one long year
he has been done with the sufferings of life. My prayer is that I may
meet him in Heaven."

August 10th, 1865, Selma, Alabama

Dear Sister: It is with pleasure that I sit down this mornin to
let you know that I am well at the presant and hope that this
will find you the same. I havent nothing of importence to write
at this time. The wether is not so hot as it has bin for some
time. I expect that Will is making it pay about this with his

watermelons. *Thare is plenty of melons & peaches down hear yet but apels is a scarse artical in this part of the department. Thare is a good meney figs but I dont like them till they are put up in little boxes. Mary, thare is a good meney girls in this city but as you know that I am afraid of the girls. I havent spoke to one of them yet. I was thinking of comin home in time for the Cass Co fair but I guess that I will put it off till Christmas. If we dont come then I will put it off to spring. Home bothers some of the boys heads concidrable but it dont afect mine in the least for I think that I can stay down hear and play souldier, as it is called now. Thare is no fighting now to do and we are just staing down hear and playing souldier. Mary I cant find eney thing that I can send in a letter that is nice. We haft to pay dobel price for things hear. Well Mary I beleave that I have writtin all that can think of at the presant time so no more. Your affectionate brother, Thomas Paschal To Miss Mary E. Paschal. PS. Pleas excues all bad writing and spelling and this short letter & give my respects to all enquiring friends & t y[214]. Goodbye Sister Mary.*

August 13th, 1865, Selma, Alabama

Dear Sister Mary: It is with the gratest of pleasure that I sit down this Sunday evening to write you a few lines to in form you that I am well and hope this will find you the same. Mary, as for news, that is playd out but maby I can write something that will intrest you a little for I know that your letters all ways does me. Mary, I have writen to Rachel & Thanel & Eddy & Jonny all in one letter this evening and I thought that it was your time. Mary, the men are talken a good deal about furlows but I dont think that I will aply for one for I think that if I was to get one ah those, I would want to stay. I think I can stay till

214 To You.

*my time is out & I think that you can get along without seeing
me for that short of time. It is the 13 of August and prety soon
it will be my time half out and then it will go down hill and
then I will think that my time is geting shorter. Mary, I havent
got meney corospondents but as meney as I have I try and
anser all that I get. Mary, you know that thare was some body
that told me to write. Well I wrote three or fore and she did
not anser them and I quit. I need not tell her naim. I have a
bout run out of eney thing to write so I guess that I will quit,
so no more. Yours truley, Thomas Paschal, to his sister Mary.
PS. Write soon and often but I guess that you write pretty often
eney how, that is all, so goodbye for this time, sister Mary.
With the folks that put on ares we are a marching a long with
the for and thirty stars[215].*

August 18th AD, 1865, Selma, Alabama

*Dear Sister Mary: It is with the gratest of pleasure that I sit
down this evening to anser your kind & welcome letter which I
received yesterday, dated July 7. It found me well & I hope that
this will find you the same. Thare is not much of importence
except our Capten Leiks[216] fell out of the third story of a bilding
and stove himself up considerble but I think that he will
recuver but I dont think that he will be able to comand this
Company for a good while for he had little enofe of sents and I
am afraid that he wont have eney agin. He would get botherd
& could not give the comands rite but it takes our second
Lieutenant John A Meral[217] to make things git. He is most of
a military man. That is enofe of that. Mary, thare has bin too
Reg of cavalry, one this morning & 9th Illinois. Thare was a*

---

215 Perhaps Thomas is referring to 34 states with the Union restored.
216 Captain Phillip S. Likes (47th Illinois, Co. F)
217 Lieutenant John A. Merrill.

man in the Co by the name William Paschal[218] from Fayette
County but I could not make him out eney kin to me. I saw
him at Camp Butler last spring. He has a sister by the name
of Elen Paschal[219]. I thought that he ought to be some kin but
I dident knoe that thare was some of kin. Sister Mary, I cant
tell how long that we will stay here. I would like to get a little
farther north if it was not more than 7 or 8 hundred miles.[220]
The boys are tolrable well in the Co. I have not seen eney one
that I ever saw before but the 114 and they past here one
month today on there way home. Our reg & the 12th Iowa
are doing duty hear. Mary, you must excuse this short letter
and all bad writing & spelling. It comes a little more handy
to me to write than it did when I fist came in the surves but I
dont know wither that I can write eney better or not. Mary I
have got about 20 letters home & I expect that meney more.
My time is most half out. It will be half out September 3th &
that wont be long. I must quit for this time. From your brother,
Thomas Paschal. To Miss Mary E Paschal. PS. Mary, you did
not say eney thing about Albert. I want you to speak of him &
the rest. So no more. I thank you for your letters, sister Mary.

September 5, 1865, Camden, Alabama

Dear Sister Mary: It is with pleasure that I take my pen in
hand to anser your kind letters which I recieved this morning
dated 16 & 29th. I was glad to hear from you and that you
was well & hope this letter will find you in good helth. You

---

218 William Henry Paschal (6th Illinois Cavalry, Co. A) was Thomas' third cousin. He
was born in 1834 and, upon his return to Fayette County, Illinois, married, January
9, 1868, Julia Ann Ackers. They had at least six children. Thomas' great grandfather, Isaiah Paschal I, and William's great grandfather, Thomas Paschal, were
brothers.

219 Lucy Ellen Paschal was born in 1846 and married William Trueblood on October
28, 1866 in Fayette County, Illinois.

220 700 or 800 miles north to "Cass County"?

said that Uncle Crow had sold out and was going to Napels[221].
I was sory to hear that Miss Massie had such a sore nose but
I hope that it will get well for she is a good girl or I thought so
eney way. I expect that your school will be out prety soon but
I wont be thare in time to come after you. If I am home a gin
Christmas I will think that I am doing well but I would not
care a cent. Mary, we have moved to an out away place where
we dont get our male very regular but I hope that we wont stay
hear long. Mary, you must excuse this short letter for I want to
get it in the mail to nite. I will quit for this time hoping to hear
from you soon. Good bye for this time. Yours truley, Thomas
Paschal To his Sister Mary Paschal

Sept 12th, 1865, Camden, Alabama

Dear Sister Mary: It is with pleasure that I sit down this
morning for the purpos of writing you a few lines to inform
you that I am well & hope that you are the same. Sister, I cant
talk very well with pen & ink but I think that if I was thare I
could talk [to] you a noif. I dont expect to be in Illinois mutch
before spring but we ant a doing eney good here as I can see. I
have an ideah that it is the oficers falt that we stay down here.
They are a geting big pay and they would rather be here than
at home. The last letter that I receved from you was dated
Aug 29th. Mary I suppose that your school will soon be out
but I cant get thare to come after you so you will haft to get
some other arrangments to get home. Mary, the girls are very
fraid of the yankes as they call them. Thare was one came
in town the other day and she did not know that thare was
eney souldiers in town and she started an ran and ran till she
couldent run eney longer and she got to an old siteson[222] and

221 Naples, Illinois

222 citizen

she was all most gone up[223]. Well, Mary, we are quarterd in an old hotell but I dont like this way a bording at an hotell where I haft to do my own cooking. I can have my choice to do my own cooking or have an negro to do it but I dont want eney darky in my cooking. We hear that the negroes are a going in to Illinois. When you write tell me if it is so or not. I dont beleave that it is. If they are thare a bout Beardstown when I get [back] I think that they will haft [to] git. Mary, I will quit for this time, so no more this time. Yours truley, Thomas Paschal To his sister Mary.

Sept 17th, 1865, Camden, Alabama

Dear sister Rachel[224]: It is with pleasure that I sit down this sabath evening to anser your kind letter which I received yesterday and was glad to hear from you and that you was all well. I am well at this time & hope you are the same. I have nothing of importence to write at presant. We have no news down hear at all but time pases off fast. It is the middle of September. I will soon have seven months servd & no pay yet from the goverment nor I dont expect eney untill I am musterd out and I hardley think that will be before next spring. We may get out in two or three monts but I think it doutful. I suppose that Sister Mary is home in this time. I would like to be thare a day or so with you and help you eat your vegatables but we have plenty of sweet potatoes when we go after them. I guess you know how we get them. If you dont just ask Thanel[225] and I suppose that he can form an ideah how we get them when we go out after nite with our harber sacks[226]

---

223 Maybe he means "exhausted" or "done in".

224 This is the only letter that was not written to his sister Mary.

225 Referring to Nathaniel Peters, Rachel's husband.

226 He must be referring to a "haversack," a bag in which soldiers carried their rations, as when on the march.

on. I had beter quit hinting or you will think that we hook
them. The boys are all well. Pleas excuse this short letter. No
more this time. Your brother, forever, Thomas Paschal. To Mrs
Rachel Peters

Sept 17th 1865, Camden, Alabama

*Dear Sister Mary: It is with pleasure that I sit down this
evening to pen you a few lines to let you know that I am well
an hope that these few lines will find you the same. As I have
writen to or three letters to day I have almost run out of eney
thing to write. I guess that your school is out in this time. You
wrote in your last letter that you had some noshen of teachen
this winter. Do just as you please and have all the fun that
you want & I think that if time pases off as fast the next five
monts & a half as they have this six & a half I will be home
prety soon. It may seam long to you but it dont seam very long
to me. I will quit. Hoping to hear from you soon. From your
brother Thomas. To Miss Mary Paschal*

Sept 24, 1865, Camden, Alabama

*Dear Sister Mary: It is with the gratest of pleasure that I sit
down this sabath morning for the porpos of ansering your kind
& welcom letters, one that I riceived yesterday & one that I
received Thursday. I was glad to hear from you and that you
was well. I suspose that you haft left Inden Creek* [227] *some time
a go. You spoke of going to Sister Margrets in your last letter so
I will write a letter to her to day, so if you dont get this letter
you can hear just as well. I received a letter from Bro[ther]
Joseph the other day. He was geting along well onley he had*

---

227 Indian Creek, where Mary taught at Green Meadow School, and where she would
meet her future husband, Jonathan Hobson.

bout himself a new gun & went out to try it & tied his horse to a tree and when he came back his horse had choked itself to deth. I think that was a good joak on the tree dont you. Mary, I all most forgot to say that I was well but I suppose that you would of judged that I was. Thare is rumer in Camp that we will return to Selma soon but it is not confermed yet. Mary, I cant think of eney thing to write hardley you want to hear from me often so I try to let you here from me once a weak. I write that often weather you get them or not I cant say. The boys are all well except Burns. He had a small shake of the ague[228] yesterday. Excuse this poor short little letter & I wil try & do beter the next time. You need not laugh at this scratched writing for I have nothing elce to do and am writing out of another fellows ink & you know that I must use all the ink that I can for that is the way they they do when they get my ink.[229] No more this time. From your brother, Thomas Paschal. To Miss Mary Paschal. PS. I will quit for this time hoping to hear from you soon. Good by Sister Mary

October 2, 1865, Selma, Alabama

Dear Sister Mary: It is with pleasure that I sit down this pleasant after noon to write you a few lines in anser to your kind letter which I received last nite dated Sept 7. It was all most a month coming. I was glad to hear from you and that you was well. It found me well & it leaves me the same. I dont know whear you are, weather you ar at home or at Mt. Sterling but I will direct it to Beardstown eney how. I suspose that Thanels a doing well sence they got back to the Leonard farm. I receved a letter from Sister Rachel & also one from Bro Will. Grub cant write mutch some how or rather, but

---

228 chills, fever, sweating.

229 The penmanship on this page was large with flourishes, as if purposely "using all the ink" he could.

Rachel she has got some small sheats so that she can fill them up. Sister wrote that she thought that if I was thare that me & Thanel would have a nice time maken hay, but she nead not think that for work I have forgot how. I suspose you see by the communcion of my letter that we have got back to Selma. We have a nice [camp] hear. I was on duty to day I was detailed to paleace the camp but I playd it sharp. I prest in an old Buck Negro to do the work & I bost[230] the job. Mary, before I sit down to write it seames as if I could write a grate long letter, but when I get at it I cant think of eney thing hardley. All the boys are well. The weather is pleasant hear now. If the nites gets mutch colder I will be a looking for frost pretty soon. Mary, it is almost time to get supper & I must quit. Please excuse all mustakes & bad spelling & wrtting. So no more this time. Yours truley, Thomas Paschal. To his sister Mary Paschal. PS. Give my best respects to all enquiring friends & keep a large poshen for your self. No more this time.

October 7, 1865, Selma, Alabama

Dear Sister Mary: It is with pleasure that I sit down this Sunday evening for the purpos of writing you a few lines to let you know that I am well & hope this will find you the same. I have nothing of importence to write at the presant. The wether is geting nice & pleasant down in this part of the world & I suspose that it is geting pretty cool up thare. Thare was a smaul ryett[231] in town last nite with negroes. Thare was two old darks came out of the edge of town & fired in our camp and the major got up & detailed a squad of men & tuck five of them prisnors & shot one in the hand & another in the leg, so I think that the negro will soon take the hint that they had

---

230 bossed

231 riot

better let the souldiers a lone. Mary, this is a large sheat but still I will do the best that I can for it. Mary, it seams to me that if I was thare that I could think of more to tell you than I can now but still if nothing turns up larger than a steam boat I think that I will be up thare some time next March sooner or later. That ant long, little over four monts. I want you to tell me wether it is geting cold up thare or not. I have staid down hear all the hot wether & I think that I can stay the winter prety well. Mary thare are hickry nuts & chestnuts down hear & peanuts & graps & persimons & all sorts of nuts but still if you folks gethers plenty of pecans you may save me a bushel or so. Mary, I see that I cant fill the hole sheat so I will cut it in to & write to some one elce on that peace, but it ant becuse I am scarse of paper for I have enofe of foolscap[232] *to write a week. All the boys are well. Dutch got a letter from home stating that they wer a going to leave the botom. Sister, I beleave that I have writen all that I can think of at the presant. Hoping to hear from you soon. Yours as ever, Thomas Paschal To his Sister Mary. PS. Give my best respecks to all enquiring friends & keep a large poshen for your self. No more this time. Good bye sister Mary*

October 14, 1865, Selma, Alabama

Dear Sister Mary: It is with pleasure that I sit down this evening to anser your kind letter which I received this morning. I was glad to hear from you & that you was well but was sory hear that Emlin[233] *and the little shaver*[234] *& also Margret was sick but hope that they are all well before this time. I am well & hope this will arive safe & find you in good*

---

232 "Foolscap" is paper typically 16" X 13" and so called because of a watermark of a fool's cap formerly applied to such paper.

233 Emlin Dunn Paschal, William's wife. (*Dunn)

234 Harriett Ellen Paschal was six months old.

helth. I have no news of mutch importance to write. I have bin
out in the country last weak about 25 miles for the purpos of
aresting some men that had captured our goverment teames.
We started at six a clock in the evening & road till 12 in the
nite and came up on the men. Tuck 15 prisnors & some of
them got away. Them that ran we shot at but it was so dark we
did not hit eney of them. It was the first horse that I had rode
sence I left home & you had better gues that it had made me
tird. Thare is a goverment sale in town now. Just tell them folks
if they want good horses & muels to just cum down but they
had beter huray for I expect it will close in too or three days.
I dont know wether to direct [this letter] to Mt. Sterling or to
not but I guess I will direct to Beardstown. The boys in the
Company are generly tolrable well. Mary in a little over four
monts & then I expec to start for Illinois but not mutch sooner
tho I dont expect. Well Sister, I will quit for this time. Hoping
to hear from you soon. No more this time. From your brother,
Thomas Paschal. To Mary E Paschal. Goodbye for this time.

October 16, 1865, Selma, Alabama

Dear Sister Mary: It is with pleasure that I sit down this
morning for the purpos of ansering your letter which I received
this morning. I am well and hope this will find you the same.
I was sorry to hear that Margret & Aleck wer both sick but I
hope that they are both well before this time. Mary, I received
a letter from you last Saturday but did not anser it in time to
get is in the male that nite and was on duty yesterday, and this
morning I received another and so I will anser it & send them
both in one envelop. Mary yesterday was the first time that I
have bin on duty on Sunday sence I have [been] in the surves.
Sister I think that ho ever stated that the 47 Reg was at Springfield was badley mustaken for I have bin with Reg almost all
the time and the Reg is hear yet and no sines of leaving as I

see.[235] *Mary the pay master is in town but weather he is going to pay us off or not I cant say but I will know when I write a gane. If I am paid maby I will get a picture and send to you but they cost so much down hear. I look pretty mutch as I did when I left home as far as I can see by looking in the glass. Please excuse all bad spelling & writing & all mustake and I will quit. Hoping to hear from you soon, I remain your afectionate Brother Thomas Paschal. To his sister Mary E. Paschal. PS. Give my love to all enquiring friends and keep a large poshen for your self. No more this time. From Mr Thomas Paschal Co F 47 Reg Ill Vol Infan.*

November 1, 1865, Selma, Alabama

Dear Sister: It is with pleasure that I sit down this evening to write you a few lines in anser to your kind & welcome letter which I received this morning. It found me well and I hope these few lines will find you and the rest of the famley the same. I was glad to hear that Sister was geting better. Well Sister I am on guard to day at the prison or guard hous which ever you may call it. I am on the third releaf and when I had stad my too hours I came to camp for my diner and the boys had it redy. After I eat, A. Dock[236] gave me your letter and I thought that I had beter anser it before I went back. Sister, that box that you spoke of made my mouth water but if you hant sent it before you get this letter, I can do very well with out it for I expect that it would cost a good deal and I would soon eat it. We have onions & potatoes & pickels some times. We live well enofe for souldiers. I was glad to get them stamps for I was just out but I have one greenback yet that sister Rachel sent me. Stamps is a scurse artical down hear.

---

235 It appears that someone told Mary the 47th Illinois Regiment was in Springfield, Illinois.

236 Referring to Abel Cottrell.

What few that they have they sell them at five cents a peace.
Cottrel is seting hear a working at a ring and I am rather
slow a writing and he saes for you to eat an apple for him.
Mary, one of our feifers dide last Saturday and I was at his
bering on Sunday and thare was a young lady thare and she
had tears in her eyes and fixed an nice bokey of flours on a
souldiers grave that was kild hear when this place was taked.
I dont know but I think that she allways was union. I think a
grate deal more of her than I do of a cupel of girls that was a
walken along the street when we first came hear. The flag was
out at Head Quarters and when they saw it they twisted up
ther nose and went on the other side of the street. I must quit
prety soon for the Sargent wants me to go back but I told him
to go on and I would be at my post a gin at four oclock. Mary
I think that if I count things write it is all most 8 monts sence
I left home, four more and then I will begin to talk about
coming home. Mary I think that it must be tolrable cool up
thare by this time for it is very nice wether down hear. Pleas
excuse this poor letter and I will write a gane soon. I will quit.
Hoping to hear from you soon. From your brother, Thomas.
To Miss Mary E. Paschal. No more this time.

November 8th, 1865, Selma, Dallas County, Alabama

Dear Sister: It is with pleasure that I sit down this evening to
pen you a few lines to let you know that I am well & hope this
will find you the same. I received your letter this morning, date
27th. I was glad to hear from you & that you was well. I was
glad to hear that Sister was beter & I hope that she will be well
by the time that you get this. I have no news of importance to
write at the presant. Every thing is quiet in Selma. Thare is but
one Regment hear & that is ours. You wanted to know wether
I had mutch fun or not. I have no fun in particquilar. We have
a rite smart of sport. Time pases off fast down hear. I have

bin on duty every third day for a good while but I dont know wether the duty will be so heavy or not for they are a going to send the men that is in the guard house to Montgomery to have a court marshere. Mr. Cox from Mt. Sterling got a letter from his wife this morning, date 28th, and sade that it was a snowing thare. We have not had no snow yet but we have had a nice frost. I have writen all most all that I can think of at this time but I'll try and do beter the next time. No more from your brother, Thomas Paschal. To Miss Mary E. Paschal. Hoping to hear from you soon, good bye.

November 17, 1865, Selma, Alabama

Dear Sister Mary: It is with pleasure that I sit down this evening to answer your kind letter which I received the other day. I was glad to hear from you and that you was well. I am not very well this afternoon I have the headache. I have nothing of importance to write at the presant. Mary, we was pade off four monts pay the fifthteenth of this month and I will send you some in the letter. If you get it I want you spend it for what ever you want. You have bin writing for me to send my photograph. I could get it now but it ant but a little over three monts till I will be home if nothing hapens more than I no of. The boys are all rite. Every thing is lovely in camp. You must ecuse this short letter and I will try and do better the next time and that wont be long. I will send you 15 dollars in this letter. Wether it goes or not I will risk it eney how. I will quit for this time. Hoping to hear from you soon I remain, your loving brother, Thomas Paschal.

To Miss Mary E. Paschal. PS. Write soon and give me all the news in general.

November 30th, 1865, Selma, Alabama

Dear Sister Mary: It is with pleasure that I sit down this eveing to write you a few lines to let you know that I am well & hope these few lines will find you the same. I have no news of importance to write at the presant. I rote you a letter the other day and sent 15 dollars in it. Weather it goes or not and I will send 10 in this and risk it. Mary I did think that I would be at home on Christmas but I guess it is played out. I would like to be thare very mutch but I will make the best of it down hear with the Southern people a playing souldier but three more monts will bring me a little nearer Illinois if nothing hapens more than I no of at the presant. Thare was a man killed in Co K yesterday by accadent. Thare was a man in Co E a farting with his gun and it was loaded and he did not know it and went to snap a cap and it went off and shot this man through the body and he dide in a few hours.[237] Thare has bin one man dide with the small pox in the Reg and thare is to or three more cases I beleave but they hant eney tuck them in our Co & I hope that they wont. I am very particqular wher I go around the Regement. I have not had a letter from you for allmost too weeks but looking for one every day. I hardley know wher to direct this to, Mt Sterling or to Beardstown. I hope that you will have a good time if you go to Virgenia[238] this winter. I would like to be thare and to go with you very mutch. I must bring my letter to a close. Hoping to hear from you soon. Pleas excuse all mustakes and bad writing and spelling. No more this time. From your loving Brother, Thomas. To Miss Mary Paschal.

---

237 Although the soldier from Company E who was "farting" around with his gun remains unknown, the soldier killed from Company K was Pvt. William Deselms of Steuban, Illinois who died on Nov. 29, 1865, in Selma from a gunshot wound. (*Deselms)

238 Virginia, Cass County, Illinois. Since both of Mary's parents were dead, perhaps she was planning to celebrate Christmas with her grandfather, Isaiah Paschal, who lived in Virginia, Illinois.

December 21st 1865, Selma, Alabama

Dear Sister Mary: It's with pleasure that I sit down this evening for the purpos of ansering your kind & very welcom letter which I received this morning. It found me well & I hope that this short letter will find you the same. I was glad to hear that the folks had got well agane. I beleave that all the smallpox has got about well. I have no news of importence to write at the presant. Well Sister it is a geting prety hard work for me to write a letter for thare is not eney thing new agoing on at all. Sister Mary, I hope that you will have a good time this Christmas. It is onley four days more. I will be on duty tomorow & and then I wont be on till after Christmas. I allso received a letter from D. T. Treadway this morning. They was all rite thare. I beleave that he was helping Grub geather corn. It is very nice weather down hear for the time of year. The trees ar nice and green, all so the grass and thare is nice flours yet in yards. The boys ar all rite. I beleave a little over too monts and then if nothing hapens more than I knew of I will come marching home agane. This year has slipt off very fast to me. I dont know how it has to you. It dont seam long sence last Christmas. Mary, we have fine times down hear a playing ball. The major & the adjutent & the captains & the Lieut all come out and play, as well as the privets[239]. Mary, I done a job of tayloring yesterday. I put pockets in my overcoat. I put them in in stile. I went down in town and got 2 yards of tape and bound them and put some girley ficksings[240] on for stile. I thought that if you had a holt of it you could do it a little better than I could, but still it does me first rate. I can sew firstrate but when the washing comes I ant thare. I hant done mutch of that. I hire a negro wench to wash for me but I dont want eney of thare cooking in mine.

---

239 Union soldiers are credited with introducing the relatively new sport of baseball to the South.

240 Maybe, "girlish fixings for style."

Well Mary, I will quit for this time. I will wind up hoping to hear from you soon. No more this time. From your Brother, Thomas Paschal To his Sister Mary E. Paschal

December 25th, 1865, Demopolis, Alabama

Christmas Presant. Sister Mary: It is with pleasure that I sit down this morning to pen you a few lines to let you know that I am well and hope this will find you the same. Well Sister, Christmas has found me a good ways from home. I hope that you ar a having a good time while I am a way down here. Christmas is no more than eney other day with me but I think that if I was up thare I could have a good time. Sister if you are wher eney of the girls is that I am aquainted with when you get this, please tell them that I wish them a happy Christmas & New Years allso. Sister, I know not wher you are today but I spect that you are at some of the relatives a flying around to get dinner redey. At least I know that I must be at that business pretty soon for I am cook this week. Well, Sister, by the heading of my letter you will see that we have made a move back to Demopolis. We came down hear the 23th and I wish that I was back to Selma for it is very muddy at this place but we have beter quarters down hear and less duty, but I dispise the mud. Thare ar four Companys of our Reg hear & the remander is still at Selma. The 11th Missouri was there a doing duty but they was orderd to Memphis to quiet a negro ryett. I know not wether we will haft to go back to Selma or not but I hope not unless they ficks the bridge over the Cahaba river. Well I have bin botherd a little with a Corporel that is drunk. He is a firstrate fellow. It is the first time that he has got drunk sence he has bin with the Co and I hope that it will be the last for I dispise drunk men. Mary, the nearest that I ever was drunk was a bout a month a go. I did not feal very well and went down in town and got a

*bottel of Hosteters bitters and tuck a prety good snort and it
made me feal kinder like a fool, but I soon got over it. Well
Sister I have had my dinner but I did not have as good one as
I have had on Christmas but it done very well for a souldier.
Well Mary as long as it is Christmas I am puting on a little
stile. I have got on a paper collar & my new vest but I have
not got on my new blouse for it is warm enouf for me to go
in my shirt sleeves. Sister, you rote to me in a letter once that
it was ill maners to write [on the] blank side of a sheat but I
am not afraid of insulting you. But I will wind up shortley.
Sister, I am a enjoying myself finely down hear in this woods
country but you know that I woud rather be thare than hear
on this day. While I have bin writing I received a letter from
Sister Rachel. They wer well. She sade that she had saw Miss
Nannie Massie*[241] *the Monday before she rote on the 10. I was
also glad to hear from her. Well I must quit and anser Sister
Rachels letter, so no more this time from your loving Brother,
Thomas. I wish you a happy Christmas, Sister.*

January 1st, AD, 1866, Demopolis, Alabama

*Dear Sister: It is with the gratest of pleasure that I sit down
this New Years morning to answer your kind & very welcome
letter which I received day before yesterday but thought that I
would not answer it till 1866. It found me well and this leves
me the same and I hope that these few lines will find you the
same. This is a very disagreable day for the time of year. The
wind is in the north and it is a raining and the mud is about
a fut deep hear. Thare has bin but little cold weather down
hear yet but I suspose that it has bin about as cold as it ever
gets in the section of the country. I have nothing of impor-*

---

241 Nannie was probably a nickname for one of the daughters of Henderson and
Martha Massie of Virginia, Illinois. They had three daughters who were close to
Tommy's age.

*tance to write at the presant but think I will in the corse of a
month or so. Mary, this is a going to be a very dull day for me
for it is a raining so that I dont like to go up in town and if
I was to thare is nothing to see for it is about such a place as
Verginia[242], onley Verginia has yalow mud and this has white.
I know very well what I dun last New Years. I sit around the
house till 2 o clock and then went to Sabath School but as this
is Monday, I guess that I will not go to day. I rote you a letter
at Christmas, Mary. You nead not look for more than a dozen
more letters from me while I am in Alabama. I have nothing
more to write so I will quit and draw rashens. I will quit,
hoping to hear from you soon, so no more this time. From your
loving brother,   Thomas. Co F 47 Reg Ill Vol. To his Sister
Mary. Good Bye. This is a New Years Presant.*

On January 21, 1866, the Regiment was mustered out at Selma, Alabama and ordered to Springfield, Illinois, where it received final pay and discharge. Adjutant General's Report.

Samuel Thomas Paschal married Anna Wylder on November 22, 1877, and lived the remainder of his life on his farm in Morgan County, Illinois. Of his three children, his daughter, Sarah Lois Paschal, lived to adulthood, and married Wilbur Williams. Sarah and Wilbur's three children still lived on or near the family farm in the 1990s. Thomas and Anna Paschal are buried in Diamond Grove Cemetery, Jacksonville, Illinois. His grave marker reads simply: "Thomas Paschal (1848-1926) Co. F, 47th Reg. Ill. Inf."

---

242 Virginia, Illinois.

Tommy Paschal's grave in Diamond Grove Cemetery, Jacksonville, Illinois. Tommy is buried next to his wife Anna Wylder. Also buried in this cemetery are Tommy's sister Rachel Paschal Peters and his brother William "Old Grub" Paschal.

Part Five

The Love Letters to Mary Paschal

from Pvt. Thomas M. Cuppy,
Third Illinois Cavalry

Photograph courtesy of the author.

Mary Elizabeth Paschal.

Private Thomas M. Cuppy was sweet on Mary Elizabeth "Mollie" Paschal, the sister of Newton and Tommy. It is easy to see why. Mary's tenderness is revealed in the few surviving letters and notes that she wrote. And like her cocky brother Newton, Mollie was "pretty good lookin' to boot."

Both the birth and the death of Thomas Cuppy remains a mystery. The 1850 census of Cass County, Illinois shows four Cuppy children living with different families. Daniel Cuppy is 20 years old, born about 1830, living with the Pratt family; Benjamin C. Cuppy is 16, living with Levi and Juliet Ream. Benjamin married Mary Howell. Christena Cuppy was 13, living with the George Tureman family; and Thomas Cuppy is 11 years old, living with the Jarrett Bridges Paschal family. Daniel Cuppy is in Sangamon County, Illinois in 1860, working as a farm laborer. He enlisted in Company C, 11th Missouri Infantry. Thomas enlisted with Company C, 3rd Illinois Cavalry at Camp Butler on August 19, 1861.

Since Thomas Cuppy lived with Mary Paschal's Uncle Jarrett, he took to calling her his cousin. But they were not related. His somewhat awkward letters to Mary reveal his affection and longing for her. During his short time as a soldier Cuppy saw plenty of action in Arkansas, Missouri and Mississippi. He also went on a mission to recover stolen horses; guarded members of his own regiment who were taken prisoners after refusing to do artillery duty; and, most surprisingly, served as the orderly for Col. Grenville Mellen Dodge.

Grenville Dodge was a distinguished American. Wounded at the Battle of Pea Ridge in Arkansas he eventually attained the rank of major general and commanded the XVI Corps during Sherman's Atlanta Campaign. Fort Dodge, Kansas was named in his honor. After the war he became a member of the U.S. House of Representatives. But Dodge's greatest claim to fame was his role in the construction of the transcontinental railroad. Dodge was the chief engineer for the Union Pacific and during his long career was credited with the surveying of some 60,000 miles of railway tracks in America.

Thomas Cuppy must have been an amiable and competent young man to be assigned as the orderly for Col. Dodge, who became a brigadier general during the time that Cuppy served him.

During most of the spring and summer of 1862 Thomas Cuppy and the 3rd Cavalry battled Confederate forces in northern Arkansas. "Starving and famishing for water," according to the Adjutant General's Report (AGR), they staggered into the Union stronghold of Helena, Arkansas on July 15th, 1862. However, the AGR reported that for the 3rd Cavalry, "The long stay at Helena proved to be demoralizing and disastrous. The place was sickly, from malaria and bad water, and the men languished with disease and inactivity."

In fact, the 3rd Cavalry "languished" in Helena for over five months, from July 15th until December 23rd. In September Cuppy was sent to a hospital in St. Louis. He was likely suffering from malaria. After a month-long stay he returned to his regiment and was with them when they

Photograph courtesy of the Library of Congress.

General Grenville Dodge.

joined "the forces moving on Vicksburg, under the command of Major General W.T. Sherman." (AGR) In fact the regiment was splintered and served as both escorts and cavalry units in both the 13th Corps (under Major General John A. McClernand) and the 15th Corps under Sherman. On January 28, 1863, Cuppy "left sick on a hospital boat near Vicksburg, Mississippi." He was never heard from again.

The 114th Illinois was also serving under Sherman and consequently Newton Paschal attempted to report on Cuppy's wherabouts to his clearly concerned sister Mary. Newton mentions in several letters that he has made "numerous inquiries" into the whereabouts of Cuppy. He dutifully reports that Cuppy left on a sick boat in letters dated Feb. 15th, July 27th and August 28th. He tells his sister that no one in Cuppy's regiment, including his officers, knew what had become of him. Finally, in a letter dated December 5, 1863, nearly a year after Cuppy left Vicksburg, Newton reluctantly concludes, "It is the general supposition of all that he is dead."

If Cuppy had indeed contracted malaria then it is likely that he eventually succumbed from the disease. He may have died on the hospital boat and was buried in an unmarked grave somewhere along the Mississippi River. One thing is certain: The girl he left behind in Beardstown spent the rest of her life wondering what became of the young man who thought of her as an angel. With so many young men from Cass and Morgan Counties killed or otherwise afflicted, both mentally and physically, by the war, Mary Paschal eventually accepted a proposal of marriage from Jonathon Hobson, a man 20 years her senior; a man untarnished by the horrors of war.

In the second of two letters from Cuppy that were preserved by Mary Paschal we read of "a proposition" made by Mary to Thomas. But it is unclear as to the nature of that proposition for which Cuppy was "feeling grateful." His letters are rambling and at times a bit incoherent. His spelling is bad but his penmanship was superb. And he does try to show a sense of humor. It is unfortunate that more of the Cuppy-Paschal correspondence was not preserved. We will never know the full extent of Mary's feelings toward him, but Cuppy comes across as a lonely, confused young man who is clearly in love with the lovely sister of Newton and Tommy Paschal.

June 7th 1862

Friendship

Dear Cousin,

*With pleasure it is this eavening that I drop you a few lines
in answer to your kind letter which I received on 4 inst. O
Jeruselam if I wasent the best. Well I don't know how to
express myself but the long and short of it was I did not care
whether I eat supper or not. Well Mollie I have carried the
joke this fur. Ill give you the rest of it. We had nothing to eat
on that day but we don't care for I eat when I can get it. Well
stop Cuppy you must make some apoligies (is that spelt right)
for writing such foolishness as this.*

*Well Mollie I am a soldier now. O yes I forgot to tell you that
I was well and in good spirits but I need not tell you that
for you know that by the way I write. Well Mollie I must
tell it to you just how I am getting along. I am pretty well
and enjoying a great deal better health than beauty. For
you know as well as me that I am pretty. That is if you call
an Arab pretty for I am black ragged and saucy and don't
care whether school keeps or not so I get something to EAT.
Excuse me Mary and I will quit writing foolishness (but I just
wanted to show you that I was in good spirits).*

*Well dear Mollie the perusal of your kind letter afforded me
much pleasure for I never expected to read a letter written by
the hand it was. I am sorry to hear that you wrote to me and
I did not get it and also that I had wrote to you the second
time and you have not received but the one. The reason I
wrote the second time was I received no answer for so long
that I thought perhaps you did not get the first one. I wrote
three letters about two months ago one to uncle*[243] *and one*

---

243 This uncle is probably his benefactor, and Mary's actual uncle, Jarrett Bridges Paschal.

to Brother[244] and one to my little you know I guess for I don't and I have not received any answer yet. So I have come to the conclusion that Mary thinks more of me than any of them good for I do not intend to write to them until they write to me if it is a whole week from now.

Well dear Mary I will try to tell you where I am at the present time. Hellow! Here!! My paper is about to run out but I think I can interest you so I will fill a part of another page for I wish to tell you where and how we are situated.

Thomas M. Cuppy

To Miss Mary E. Paschal[245]

Part two of the June 7, 1862, letter from Thomas M. Cuppy to Mary Paschal:

We are at present between White River and Red the distance about 40 miles and we are about halfway between.[246] This morning our pickets were drove in by the enime and we was called up into line of battle on foot and it as dark as you please but we was ordered in a few minutes to saddle up and mount and was kept in that position unitl daylight and still no emime came. Then we dismounted and our company (well our regiment and one batery is called a fling brigade[247]) was marched off to the batery to take the canineers prisoners for

---

244 The brother could be Daniel Cuppy who was a member of the 11th Missouri Infantry.

245 The signature and salutation at the end of this letter was decorated with flourishes and hundreds of tiny dots of ink to make both of their names look as though they were written together in the stars.

246 The 3rd Illinois Cavalry was in northern Arkansas engaging in skirmishes with enemy cavalry. They reached Batesville, Arkansas on June 11th and followed the White River to Jacksonport and finally Helena where they began a long encampment.

247 Flying brigade.

they refused to serve. The reason they did not like to serve was they belonged to cavalry and was on detached service and they did not like the artilery and I have been guarding them all day until about an hour ago. And our regiment and fourth Iowa Cavalry and the fifth Mousure[248] cavalry are all about six miles from camp skirmishing with the (enemy) this eavening but let them for I am writing to one who is dear to me and I can fight tomrrow and no doubt but I will have to do it.

We are expecting an attack every hour. The main body of the enemy is about eighteen miles from us and they are advancing on us but let them come for we can whip all the rebles in the south if they will not come to fast. Well Mary I am afraid this potion of my letter will not interest you but hoping it will I send it for perhaps it will be the last time I will handel a pen but I shall trust God and keep my powder dry.

O that I could be at preer[249] meeting at the old school where but I thank God that he has kept you all together and has spared me and pray that I may be permitted to join you some time in songs of praise. O prey for me the prairs of Gods children availeth me. Mary I feel loth to quit but I have written to much now. I gave your respects to Joseph[250] and Mr. Richards[251] that is all that I could spare. So I will close my epistal by asking you to write immediately for if you knew the good that it does me I believe you would write almost before you read the letter. Excuse all mistakes for I am a soldier. Give my love to all the friends reserving a good potion for yourself.

T. M. Cuppy To: Miss Mary E. Paschal. Goodby Dear

---

248 Missouri.

249 Prayer.

250 Joseph Barwick of Arcadia, Illinois was a private in Company C.*

251 William Richard of Beardstown was a corporal for Company C.

This final letter from Thomas Cuppy was written in Helena, Arkansas. Perhaps he was already suffering from malaria. He certainly sounds a bit incoherent or even feverish at times. The letter was not signed, but if Cuppy did find some paper "to write a little more" it was not included with this partial letter preserved by Mary.

Photograph courtesy of the Arkansas History Commission.

Helena, Arkansas during the Civil War was prone to flooding as is evidenced by the picture from 1864. Malaria was widespread among the Union soldiers stationed there.

August 16, 1862

Friendship

Dear Miss,

Feeling grateful to you for the proposition made by yourself. You may find a few lines written by one who thinks he knows who he is writing to and one he would give a world to see. One that his whole delight was placed on but in after days was turned out in the world alone where you see him standing. Yet he it is you are coming with now. Mary I am thankful that there is one at home praying for me.

I received a letter from you the other day that afforded me a perusal of the same much pleasure to a once broken harted. O it will not do for me to dwell here for I perceive if I allow myself I will get to sentimental for you. So I must govern myself and keep quiet. I do thank you for the kind encouragements sent me. Pray for our country for the prayers of the religious availouth much.

Many long hours do I spend in the silent grove often on my bed of rest and many a time when I have been on my piket post at the dead hour of night O often do I flatter myself with the thought that I may enjoy her presence once more. Could I be assured of this!! Look out I expect I am getting to sentimental again my dear Mary. You should not have offered me the privaledge for I will speak my sentiments to a little extent. I hope you will not take offense. I hope not for I would not for the world. I find someone remarking some on my beauty. Well I am astonished to think that there is one. O is it not flattery? Well I'll say it is not and strike the one that made that remark by saying dito to her and adding the constructions to it I think I will have to come and see her. O happy thoughts.

Dear Mary the most cheering I have embraced for many long days though perhaps the most disgusting you could read or think about but I hope not. I wish I were up at your house to help you eat that light bread but never mind I have plenty of hard tack for I expect Misses M. Paschal would think. O dear run out of paper and not half done writing. I must write a little more so excuse me dear Mary.

Addendum

Adkins
Amos D. Adkins was born about 1841 in Cass County, Illinois, the son of William W. and Barbara (Miers) Adkins. The father was born in Tennessee, the mother in Kentucky. Amos was the oldest of at least four children: James (born 1842); Henry (born 1845), and Martha (born 1848).

Ayers
Thomas Ayers was born about 1838 in Cass County, Illinois, the second of eight children of Thomas and Matilda Ayers, natives of England and South Carolina, respectively. Before entering the war, Thomas had been a blacksmith. His siblings, all born in Illinois, were: Benjamin (born 1836); James (born 1840); Mary (born 1842); Sarah (born 1845); William (born 1847); John R. (born 1850), and Margaret (born 1853).

Barwick
Joseph Barwick was born in 1845 in Indiana, the son of Joseph Barwick, Sr. (born 1816), a minister, and his wife, Elizabeth. Joseph Jr. died July 4, 1915, and is buried in the Wyuka Cemetery in Lincoln, Nebraska.

Berry
James Berry was born February 16, 1839, in Cass County, Illinois, the son of James and Sinah (Taylor) Berry. He married Lucy A. Paschal (born 1842), daughter of Greenhill and Sarah (Deweber) Paschal on September 18, 1860. They were the parents of seven children: James H. Berry (born November 9, 1862); Nellie Mae Berry (born December 23, 1867); Louis Martin Berry (born October

3, 1869); Thomas Lee Berry (born October 5, 1871); Edward R. Berry (born June 7, 1874); Emma A. Berry (born November 12, 1876); and Leonard Row Berry (born May 4, 1880). Sometime around 1890, they moved to Warren County, Iowa. James Berry died there on January 3, 1909, and Lucy died in 1901. They are both buried in the Indianola Cemetery, Indianola, Warren County, Iowa.

Blanford   James C. Blanford was born in 1846. He is shown in the 1880 federal census living in Cass County, Illinois with his wife, Mary, and daughter, Nettie, aged 7.

Boemler   Lewis Boemler was born in 1843 in Illinois, the second of eight children of Henry and Mary Boemler. His siblings were: George (born 1841); Henry (born 1845); Henrietta (born 1848); Charles (born 1850); Amelia (born 1852); Mary (born 1855), and Julius (born 1856).

Brown   Elizabeth "Betsy" Brown, native of North Carolina, was the mother of at least nine children as follows: Calvin (born 1829); James (born 1831); William L. (1833); George A. (born 1836); Ellen (born 1837); Thomas H. (born 1838); Levi (born 1840); Rachel (born 1842); Stephen C. (born 1845), and John H. (born 1850). They were neighbors of the Coleman Paschal family. It was with several of the Brown brothers that Newton travelled to Nebraska in 1859. At least James and Levi remained in Nebraska after Newton returned to Illinois. Thomas H. Brown was a member of the 114th Regiment, Company D. Levi N. Brown enlisted on October 15, 1862, with the rank of Corporal in Co. C, 2nd Nebraska Cavalry, died of "brain fever" at Florence, Nebraska on November 9, 1862, and was buried in Mount Vernon Cemetery, Peru, Nebraska.

Burns   Charles E. Burns was born in July 25, 1842, in Springfield, Illinois, the son of Thomas and Eleanor (Craig) Burns. The father was born in Maryland and the mother in New York. There were at least three other siblings: Margaret E. (born 1836); Thomas J. (born 1838) and Benjamin F.

(born 1849). Charley married Caroline Brown, daughter of Samuel and Elizabeth Brown, natives of England, on July 25, 1869, in Cass County and became the parents of Eleanor E. "Nellie," Benjamin F., Russell C. and Lida M.

Cottrel

Abel F. Cottrel was born in 1839 in Indiana, the son of Caleb and Ann B. Cottrel. Caleb Cottrel was born in Virginia and Ann was born in Ohio. Abel was a printer by trade, and his brother Edward Cottrel, who was three years older, was trained as a cooper. He had a sister, Nancy A., born in 1848. Abel married Amanda A. Shafer in Cass County on December 3, 1863. The minister who performed the ceremony was Jarrett Bridges Paschal, an uncle of Thomas and Asa Newton Paschal. Thomas referred to Abel by the nickname "Dock."

Cuppy

The 1850 census of Cass County, Illinois shows four Cuppy children living with different families. Daniel Cuppy is 20 years old, born about 1830, living with the Pratt family; Benjamin C. Cuppy is 16, living with Levi. and Juliet Ream. Benjamin married Mary Howell; Christena Cuppy was 13, living with the George Tureman family; and Thomas Cuppy is 11 years old, living with the Jarrett Bridges Paschal family. Daniel Cuppy is in Sangamon County, Illinois in 1860, working as a farm laborer. He enlisted in Company C, 11th Missouri Infantry. Thomas Cuppy apparently died sometime around January, 1863, after enlisting in the Third Illinois Cavalry, Company C.

Deselms

William T. Deselsm, of Timber, Peoria County, Illinois, was the son of James Deselms and Mary Anne Addy. Six of James and Mary's children preceeded them in death, including Washington Deselms who died from wounds as a member of Company I, 32nd Illinois, on October 14, 1862. Son, William Deselms, Company K, 47th Illinois, died from a wound suffered when a fellow soldier from Company E accidentally shot him on November 29, 1865. Most of the Deselms are buried in the Maple Ridge Cemetery, Mapleton, Peoria County, Illinois.

Downing   David Nelson Downing was born in Missouri in 1837, the son of David R. and Catherine Downing, both natives of Kentucky. Other siblings in the family, all born in Missouri, were: Nathan (born 1835); William (born 1840), and Mary (born 1842). David died at Duckport, Louisiana on May 23, 1863.

Dunn   John, Luke and Robert H. Dunn were the sons of Luke and Elizabeth Dunn of Cornwall, England. John and Caroline (Treadway) Dunn were the parents of five children: Elizabeth Dunn (born 1841); Mary Ann Dunn (born March 13, 1843-died August 27, 1930) married William Paschal on December 17, 1873, after the death of her sister Emlin; Emlin Dunn (born June 30, 1845-died September 8, 1872) married William Paschal on December 24, 1863; Sarah Dunn (born 1847); and William S. Dunn (born 1849). Many of the Dunns are buried in the Oak Grove Cemetery in Beardstown, Illinois.

Freeman   Henry D. Freeman was born January 25, 1835, the youngest of six children of Littleberry and Elizabeth (Young) Freeman, both natives of North Carolina. Littleberry Freeman was a brother of Agnes (Freeman) Paschal. Henry had five sisters: Ethinda H. (born 1822) married John McDonald; Dorinda Bernice (born January 1825) married Joseph Hunt; Almeda S. (born April 1826) married Jeremiah Cox; Parilee (born April 1829-died September 1835); and Permelia (born 1832) married first George B. Arendt and, after his death, married Hugh T. Elliott. Henry Freeman married Sophia E. Bassett, the daughter of William and Ann Bassett, on March 1, 1866, in Cass County, Illinois. They had three children: Anna Elizabeth who died April 25, 1869; Anna Bernice (born October 14, 1869) married Marcellus C. Petefish on March 22, 1893 in Cass County, Illinois. She died February 14, 1953, and is buried in Walnut Ridge Cemetery near Virginia, Illinois; and Grace Eliza, born October 30, 1871, died in 1971 at the age of 100, and is buried in Walnut Ridge Cemetery. Henry Freeman died on June 8, 1878, in Virginia, Illinois, and Sophia died 1934. Both are buried in Walnut Ridge Cemetery.

Gans   Henry Gans was born in 1838 in Pennsylvania, the second of at least six children born to Peter and Elizabeth Gans. His siblings were: Levi (born 1837); Sarah (born 1839); Hannah (born 1840); Elizabeth (born 1850), and William (born 1851). Henry married Mary F. Millner on February 7, 1867. The 1880 census shows him in Cass County, Illinois with his wife and seven children--Oscar 10, Emma 9, Harry 8, Hattie 6, Jessie 5, Mattie 3 and Maud 10 mos. He was a farmer.

Garlick   William B. Garlick was born in Illinois in 1839, the son of James and Mary Garlick. He had a sister Mary, born 1837, and a brother Joshua P., born 1838.

Harris   Martin Van Buren Harris was born about 1840 and had married Mary L. Harris, daughter of George W. and Paulina Harris in April of 1860. In the 1880 census, he is shown working as a carpenter and living with his wife and adopted son, Oscar, aged 12.

Hager   Lyman Hager was born in New Hampshire on 30 August 1828. He married Cornelia Spalding who was born in Indiana on January 15, 1838, and died December 28, 1878, leaving nine children: Rose A., Edward, Douglas, Clara, Esther, Emma, Christina, Mary and Joseph. On January 5, 1879, Lyman Hager married Annie Devlin and they became the parents of two additional children, William and Charles. Lyman died on April 20, 1896, and is buried in Beardstown's Oak Grove Cemetery.

Haywood   The Haywoods were neighbors of the Coleman Paschal family. Joseph Haywood, son of Peter and Mary Haywood, born 1846 in Cornwall, England, appears to have been a close friend of Asa Newton Paschal. Joseph's brother, John Haywood, married Caroline Harris, daughter of Joseph and Martha Harris, on December 31, 1856, and his sister, Emeline Haywood (born 27 October 1838), married Thomas Knight (born 14 August 1836 in Cornwall, England) on October 27, 1859. The 1860 census shows Joseph living with Thomas and Emeline Knight. Joseph Haywood was killed in battle on July 15, 1864, approximately one month after

Newton was captured at Brice's Cross Roads. He is buried in Beardstown's Oak Grove Cemetery.

Hitchcock   Norman S. Hitchcock was born in 1837 in Maine, the son of Albeon and Hannah Hitchcock. His father was a native of New York and his mother of Vermont. He had at least three siblings, all born in New York: William (born 1843); Martha (born 1844), and Adeline E. (born 1850). Norman is buried in the Evergreen Memorial Park, Riverside, California.

Kenchler   Edward E. Kenchler was born in 1842 in Saxony, Germany, the son of William and Christianna Kenchler. He was one of 7 children. On December 21, 1871, he married Emma Wankel, daughter of Peter and Adeline Wankel. The 1880 census shows them living in Cass County with children Charles E. 7; Richard 6, and Rudolph 4. Edward's occupation was a tinner.

Kippenberg   Richard F. Kippenberg enlisted as a 43-year-old merchant in Beardstown, Illinois. He was born in South Carolina, married Amanda Hearndon on August 8, 1847, and had two children, Mary 9 and William 7.

Kuhlman   William Kuhlman was born June 19, 1840, in Prussia, the son of Gottlieb and Mary (Markham) Kuhlman. On September 14, 1865, he married Nancy J. McLin, daughter of John and Charity McLin, born in Morgan County, Illinois on January 4, 1844. They became the parents of seven children: Ella, Elizabeth C., Clara M., Harry, Charles, Myrtle and Edgar.

Lightfoot   Joseph C. Lightfoot was the son of John and Ann Lightfoot. Other siblings were: William (born 1842); James C. (born 1844); Mary F. (born 1847); Alice (born 1852); Anna (born 1855), and Sarah (born 1857). Joseph married Martha A. Treadway, daughter of Lawson and Catherine Treadway, on March 12, 1863, in Cass County, Illinois. The 1880 federal census shows Martha A. Lightfoot, widow, with sons, John E. 15, James C. 12 and Joseph R. 8.

Lindsley   Erastus Darwin Lindsley was from Beardstown, Illinois. He married Harriett Horn on December 25, 1850, in Cass County.

McCandless DeWitt C. McCandless married Sarah Ann Collins on September 5, 1867. DeWitt is buried in the Hazelwood Cemetery in Springfield, Missouri.

McCarty Robert McCarty was 36 years of age when he enlisted from Beardstown, Illinois on August 11, 1862. He was born in Kentucky and before moving to Illinois had lived in Vigo County, Indiana where he pursued his trade as a miller. Remaining at home when he left for the war were his wife, Rebecca, and at least six children: Nancy (born 1848); James (born 1850); Martha (born 1852); Ross O. (born 1855); Robert (born 1858), and William (born 1860). He died at Memphis, Tennessee on December 16, 1863.

McLane Joseph Milton McLane was born about 1813 in Kentucky. Before he enlisted in the war, he was a farmer. He and his wife, Mary, had at least five children. Two sons, Joseph Milton McLane, Jr. and Riley William McLane were also members of the 114th Regiment, Company A. Other children were Henry C. (born 1844); John (born 1849) and Jonathan (born 1852). The senior Joseph McLane died at Beardstown, Illinois on February 16, 1865. Joseph M. McLane, Jr. married Emilin J. Dunn, daughter of Luke and Elizabeth Dunn, on May 26, 1870. Riley W. McLane was killed at Tupelo, Mississippi on July 14, 1864.

Maine Luther Maine was born in November 14, 1844, the son of Lodericke and Sarah (Califf) Maine. He married Ellen McKean, born March 23, 1847, the daughter of John and Nancy McKean, on February 23, 1869. They had three children, Minta, Lucas A. and Minnie. Luther died on September 12, 1944, and is buried in New Virginia Cemetery, Warren County, Iowa.

Meyer Louis Meyer was born in 1835 and had immigrated from Germany with his brother Herman. He married Eliza Nicholson on August 18, 1856 in Cass County, Illinois.

Moore Thomas Moore was born in February 1838, the son of William and Kesiah Moore, and one of at least ten children. The 1880 census shows Thomas, a farmer, living with his wife Matilda

J., born February 1845, and their children, William R. 11, Miriam C. 10, John G. 8, Calvin S. 6, Millard M. 4, and Dollie 11 mos. They later moved to Washington County, Kansas.

Nicholson   William Nicholson was born in 1838 in England, the son of Charles and Mary Nicholson, both natives of England. William was one of at least seven children, including: Eleanor (born 1829); John (born 1832); Thomas (born 1834); Samuel (born 1843); Rebecca (born 1846), and Charles H. (born 1849).

Pedigo   Urban Pedigo was born in 1834 in Kentucky. He was married to Mary Catherine Paschal, daughter of Green Hill and Sarah (Deweber) Paschal. Urban died at Duckport, Louisiana on May 23, 1863. His brother, William Taylor Pedigo, married Mrs. Emmaline Williams on November 15, 1860, in Cass County.

Phillippi   Victor J. Phillippi was born in Illinois in 1842, the son of Pompeius and Carlena Louisa (Richelmann) Phillippi, natives of Germany. They lived near Arenzville in Cass County. Victor had at least five siblings: Louisa (born 1835); Anna (born 1837); Herman E. (born April 23, 1844); Bertha A. (born 1846), and Charles (born 1850).

Rhineberger   George M. Rhineberger was born about 1836 in Virginia.

Sackett   Orange E. Sackett was born in 1842 in Ohio, the son of Eligor and Patty Sackett. His siblings were: Susan (born 1839); Flora C. (born 1844), and Ella M. (born 1848). Orange is buried in the Fairview Cemetery in Council Bluffs, Iowa.

Saylor   Abraham J. Saylor was born in 1836 in Tennessee. He married Adeline Cire, daughter of John L. and Catherine Cire, native of Hesse-Darmstadt, Germany, on December 26, 1864, in Cass County, Illinois. Abraham and Adeline, with daughter Annie C., 11 yrs. old, are shown in the 1880 federal census in Cass County. Abraham's occupation is shown as a dealer in livestock. Saylor died March 30, 1898, and is buried Arenzville East Cemetery in Cass County, Illinois.

Schaeffer   John Morris Schaeffer was born in 1837, the son of Henry and Sophia Schaeffer. They lived near Monroe in Cass County. Other children in the family, all born in Illinois, were: Frances M. (born 1839); Eliza J. (born 1842); William F. (born 1845), and James A. (born 1847).

Schmehl   Conrad Schmehl married Catherine Stock in Cass County, Illinois on April 11, 1872. He is buried in the Evergreen Cemetery, Colorado Springs, Colorado.

Shootman   David Shootman was born in 1840, the third of at least eight children born to William and Sarah Shootman, natives of Kentucky. His known siblings were: William Jackson (born 1836); John (born 1838); Thomas (born 1842); George (born 1844); Nicholas (born 1846); Nancy (born 1848) and Patience (born 1849). The family may have moved to Missouri before the war since David served for the Union with the 11th Missouri Regiment, Company I.

Sills   Solomon Sills was born in 1842, the son of Noah and Jane Sills, both natives of Kentucky. On February 11, 1867, he married Mary Matilda Maudy in Cass County, Illinois. Woodford Sills, born 1846, brother of Solomon, enlisted in Company F, 47th Regiment. He also had a sister Nancy E., born 1844. Solomon died October 3, 1908, and is buried in La Plata Cemetery in La Plata, Missouri.

Snyder   Uriah Snyder was born in 1830, and married Harriett A. Williams in Cass County, Illinois on August 26, 1862. The 1880 census shows Uriah as a farmer, living with his wife and five children, Maria E. 13, William 12, George 8, Joseph 7 and John F. 1.

Street   Joseph E. Street, born January 24, 1840, was the son of Asa and Sarah (Cauby) Street who migrated to Lee County, Iowa from Cass County, Illinois. After his return from the war, Joseph married Martha Copp, born August 8, 1846, in Tioga County, Pennsylvania, on October 8, 1867. After their marriage, they moved to Lincoln, Nebraska and raised a family of five children: Asa Clyde (born August 23, 1860); Sylvia A. (born June 30, 1871), married William Butterfield; Frank Willis (born April 8, 1873); Pearl L. (born January 17, 1878); and Jesse A. (born August 8,

1885). Joseph died on July 10, 1925, and Martha died on June 17, 1928. Both are buried in Wyuka Cemetery in Lincoln, Nebraska.

Stuckey
Jacob S. Stuckey was born in Ohio in 1842, the 4th of seven children of Abraham and Eleanor Stuckey. His siblings were: George W. (born 1838); Susan A. (born 1845); James W. (born 1847); Abraham (born 1849); Eliza J. (born 1851), and Cynthia (born 1855). Jacob died at Memphis, Tennessee on May 23, 1864.

Taylor
Thomas Taylor married Eliza Bowen on May 24, 1859, in Cass County, Illinois. He is shown as a widower in the 1880 census with children, James, 19; Mary,16; Charles, 14; Ellen, 12; and John, 9. His occupation was saloonkeeper.

Thomas
Francis Marion Thomas, son of George Washington and Mary (Paschal) Thomas, married Margaret Hawk on March 22, 1866. They lived near Morrison, Whiteside County, Illinois.Like his father, who was named after a famous Revolutionary War hero, Francis was named after Francis Marion, "The Swamp Fox."

Treadway
Martin Treadway was born about 1839, the son of John and Rebecca Treadway. He had older brothers James (born 1832); Edward (born 1834) and Louis (born 1837). Martin married Mary Murphy on November 26, 1872. The 1880 federal census shows him in Cass County with wife Maria and daughter Lizzie 4 months. He is practicing the trade of a cooper.

Truebwasser
John Truebwasser was born in 1832 in Germany and, with his wife Caroline, was living in Cass County, Illinois in 1860. He was a carriage maker. He died on June 26, 1864.

Unland
George Frederick Unland lived in Arenzville, Cass County, Illinois. He was born in 1838 in Germany, the son of Charles and Mary Unland.

Webb
John Webb was born in 1835 in Maryland, the son of John and Eliza A. (Kahaley) Webb. The father had been born in England, the mother in Virginia. On October 5, 1858, John married Carrie Carr who died on February 2, 1862. He next

married Mary E. Baldwin on September 7, 1863.

Weddeking   John H. Weddeking married Helena Tenbick on April 19, 1866. The 1880 federal census shows him in Cass County with his wife and four children, Fred, 13; Anna, 10; George, 8; and Emma, 3. His occupation is shown as cigarmaker.

Wells   William E. "Farrell" Wells was the son of Jacob and Drusilla Wells. The 1880 federal census shows Farrell in Cass County, Illinois with his wife, Mollie, aged 33, and sons, Loren, 14 and William, 9. Farrell died on February 18, 1888. Farrell's brother, Alpheous H. Wells, was a member of the 114th Regiment, Company A, and had died during the war in St. Louis on April 10, 1862. Other siblings were: Edward, born 1841; Elizabeth, born 1844; Jacob, born 1852, and John F., born 1856. The father, Jacob, was born November 4, 1798, and died August 27, 1871; the mother, Drusilla, was born April 8, 1812, and died August 10, 1872. Members of this family are buried in Wells Cemetery in Cass County, Illinois.

Williams   Thomas H. Williams married Elizabeth Ann Way on July 2, 1860, in Cass County, Illinois

Index

Photograph by Chloe Fulton.

The author, Joe Fulton, visits the grave of his great uncle, Newton Paschal, at the Andersonville National Historic Site.

9052218R0

Made in the USA
Charleston, SC
06 August 2011